748.59 L967
Luebbering, Ken.
Gospels in glass

MID-CONTINENT PUBLIC LIBRARY
Blue Ridge Branch
9253 Blue Ridge Blvd.
Kansas City, MO 64138

BR

Consider the light streaming through the windows...
marvelleth at the priceless beauty of the glass
and at the variety of this most preciou̶̶̶̶̶̶̶̶̶̶

— Roger of Helmershausen, 1120 (̶

D1205163

Samaritan Woman at the Well, St. Joseph Catholic, Kimmswick.

Previous Page: Ascension, St. Andrew Catholic, Tipton.

Gospels in Glass:
Stained Glass Windows in Missouri Churches

Ken Luebbering
Robyn Burnett

Pebble Publishing, Inc.
Rocheport, Missouri

MID-CONTINENT PUBLIC LIBRARY
Blue Ridge Branch
9253 Blue Ridge Blvd.
Kansas City, MO 64138

BR

MID-CONTINENT PUBLIC LIBRARY

3 0001 01060382 9

Gospels in Glass: Stained Glass Windows in Missouri Churches

ISBN 1-891708-05-8 18.95

Copyright © 2000 Ken Luebbering and Robyn Burnett

All rights reserved. No part of this book may be reproduced, stored in a retrieval system, or transmitted in any form or by any means, electronic, mechanical, photocopying, recording or otherwise, without express written consent from the publisher.

Editor & Publisher: Brett Dufur
Assistant Editor: Shannon Connealy
Design & Layout: Brett Dufur
Copy Editor: Pippa Letsky

Published by Pebble Publishing, Inc.
P.O. Box 2, Rocheport, MO 65279
Phone: (573) 698-3903 Fax: (573) 698-3108
www.pebblepublishing.com

Printed by Walsworth Publishing, Marceline, Missouri, USA

Photograph on Front Cover: Mary, Detail of Annunciation, St. Joseph Catholic, Kimmswick.

Dedication

For Shiloh, Brooke and Josh—may you grow up loving the old stories.

St. George Slaying the Dragon, St. Nicholas Greek Orthodox,
St. Louis, Unique Art Glass, 1960s.

Acknowledgments

A great many people contributed to *Gospels in Glass*. The staffs at the Missouri State Archives, Western Historical Manuscript Collection, State Historical Society, and Missouri Historical Society were very helpful. Professor John Wickersham of Maryville University helped us locate stained glass in Missouri's German churches. Stephen Frei of Emil Frei Associates was extremely patient and generous in answering questions and teaching us about stained glass, particularly about the processes of design and fabrication. Robert Harmon provided invaluable insights into modern design.

Many people throughout the state contributed information about the stained glass in their communities, particularly Leslie Simpson for Joplin and David Lewis for St. Joseph. We appreciate the kindness of all the people who took time to meet us at church with a key.

Professors Sam Schnieders and Steve Wright of Lincoln University helped with equipment and advice about photography, and the staff of Full Spectrum Photo did a wonderful job processing approximately 2,500 slides.

We also wish to express our appreciation to the Missouri Humanities Council for its support of our related Internet photographic exhibit of Missouri's stained glass windows, also called *Gospels in Glass* (available at www.lincolnu.edu/~glass). Lincoln University supported our work by granting Ken a sabbatical during the 1998-99 academic year to devote time to these projects.

Contents

Chapter 1
   Perfect Gold 1

Chapter 2
   The Very Light of God: A Brief History of Stained Glass 5

Chapter 3
   Religious & Artistic Differences: Stained Glass in America 25

Chapter 4
   A Vision of God's Paradise:
         The Art of Missouri's Stained Glass 43

Chapter 5
   Light into Darkness: Iconography 59

Chapter 6
   Turning Sand into Light: The Production Process 79

Chapter 7
   Donors & Artists:
         An Example from Francis Street Methodist 87

Chapter 8
   Through Good Times & Bad:
         Missouri Stained Glass Companies 91

Chapter 9
   Of Irish Saints & Confederate Sympathizers:
         Windows into Missouri History 107

Chapter 10
   In the House of the Lord 121

Chalice, St. Nicholas Greek Orthodox, St. Louis, Unique Art Glass, 1960s.

Preface

*G*ospels in Glass is intended to provide an introduction to
Missouri's rich heritage in religious figured stained glass. The
book is not comprehensive, but the photographs represent the
geographic, artistic and denominational diversity of the state. Many
churches have interesting stories of their windows and the families that
gave them. *Gospels in Glass* tells some of those stories.

While we were researching our book *German Settlement in
Missouri: New Land, Old Ways,* we visited many German communities
around the state. We were repeatedly struck by the prominence of the
church in the small towns. Whether the church was Roman Catholic,
Lutheran, or Evangelical, it was always the most prominent building in
town, both in size and location, often perched on the highest point in the
area and rising above everything else. Of course we visited the churches,
which varied from simple architecture and decoration to neo-Gothic
buildings filled with statues, paintings and stained glass windows.

It was the windows that fascinated us the most. Who, we
wondered, was St. Kunigunda? Why was there a mouse on St.
Gertrude's staff? Why was there a spider on the chalice held by St.
Conrad? We noticed the recurrence of images: lilies, palm leaves, and
models of churches held in the hands of saints. When our book on
German immigrants was finished, we set out to answer those questions.
This book is a result of those questions. It contains a small part of what
we learned.

While we began with an interest in the symbolism of the religious
images in the windows, our research soon led us to new questions to
investigate. We noticed differences between the images found in Roman
Catholic churches and those in Protestant churches. While Catholic

churches typically have windows of saints or Biblical scenes, Protestant churches usually choose from a smaller range of familiar images such as the Good Shepherd.

There are also differences based on the ethnic make-up of the congregations. Kunigunda, Gertrude and Conrad are German saints and found only in churches with significant German-American populations. Episcopal churches, with their ties to the Church of England, contain almost all of Missouri's stained glass windows produced in England.

As we traveled the state studying and photographing windows, we were surprised by what we found in some relatively small communities. In Kennett, for example, the town center has several historic Protestant churches with early 20th century windows, while the newer Catholic church on the edge of the community contains some of the finest faceted glass windows we have seen.

Much of the best glass to be seen in Missouri's churches was produced by Missouri companies. St. Joseph, Kansas City and St. Louis all have studios today that continue to maintain the tradition of quality.

The stained glass windows of our churches can teach us lessons about our religious heritage, immigrant and community history and artistic traditions. Not only are they instructive, they are beautiful and easily accessible in every region of the state. We encourage you to visit, learn and enjoy.

Chapter 1

Perfect Gold

Arise, shine; for your light has come,
and the glory of the Lord has risen upon you.

— Isaiah 60:1

On a late autumn afternoon five centuries ago, Brother James was happy with anticipation. The painting on the test pieces of glass was completed. He inspected his work in the warm afternoon sun coming through the open door of his workshop and carefully shifted the glass into the kiln. He was confident that the new mixture of metals with which he had made the paint was the one that would produce the brilliant golden color so long desired by glaziers all over Europe when the paint was fired onto the white glass. Just as he stood up and began closing the kiln, a fellow brother appeared in the doorway.

"Father Abbot directed me to bid you begin your appointed rounds in the village," he said.

"At once," replied Brother James.

He noticed a small button had dropped from his clothes onto one of the pieces of glass, but he closed the kiln. It would have to remain until he had completed the task assigned him. Prompt obedience was more important than any piece of painted glass. Perhaps the feeling of loss he experienced was God's way of telling him he was too attached to material things. After all, what need did a monk have for a silver button? Even so, he would miss it.

His work in the village kept him away the remainder of the afternoon, and he could not return to his workshop until after the evening office of Vespers. As he brought a candle near the kiln opening he was disappointed. His new mixture had not produced the color he sought. However, as he removed the pieces of glass he was startled to find on one of them a perfect golden circle. It was the remains of his silver button. He studied it carefully. Even in the weak candle light he was certain it was the exact color he wanted. For his obedience God had rewarded him with his deepest earthly longing.

This is the story of how an Italian monk in a German monastery in the 15th century made one of the most important discoveries in the history of stained glass. It is only one of many stories in the history of stained glass. It is almost certain that James was not the first to discover how to use silver oxide to produce the golden color needed to paint halos and the blond hair of angels and beautiful saints. The fact that it is not entirely true makes it no less important. So important were the discovery and the story that Blessed James of Ulm became the patron saint of stained glass makers.

The stories of stained glass are the stories of heroes and villains, of saints and sinners, of murderers and martyrs. Some of these stories are from lands and times far from our own. They take place in ancient Rome, in Constantinople (now Istanbul in Turkey), in France and in England. They also take place in St. Louis and Kansas City, in St. Joseph and New Madrid. Sometimes they are entirely factual, sometimes they reveal truth in other ways, but they always tell us something about ourselves, about who we are and how we got that way.

Together they make up the history of stained glass windows, but they also tell us the histories of the Christian faith, of immigrants in a new land, of artists struggling to create beauty and reveal truth.

Opposite Page: Jesus Raising Jairus' Daughter, St. Paul's Episcopal, Kansas City, Jacoby, 1920s.

Young Jesus, Detail From Holy Family, St. George Catholic, Hermann, Frei, 1926.

Chapter 2

The Very Light of God:
A Brief History of Stained Glass

In the beginning God created the heaven and the earth. And the earth was without form, and void; and darkness was upon the face of the deep. And the Spirit of God moved upon the face of the waters. And God said, Let there be light; and there was light.

— Genesis 1:1-3

The stained glass that appears in churches both beautifies and instructs. The art of stained glass windows developed in Europe during the Middle Ages, probably as early as the 10th century, a time when literacy was limited to a few people and hand written manuscripts were the only form of religious publishing. Along with such popular medieval events as miracle and mystery plays, stained glass windows were a method of teaching illiterate people about their religious heritage. Even though people could not read the Bible, they could watch a play performed on the church steps or in the streets and look at a series of windows in their church that depicted the story of Christ's life from the New Testament. As they looked at a Resurrection window, they could remember the play that they had seen presented the previous Easter by one of the town guilds. Their priest would use the windows as aids in his sermons. They were an ever-present spiritual lesson to those in church.

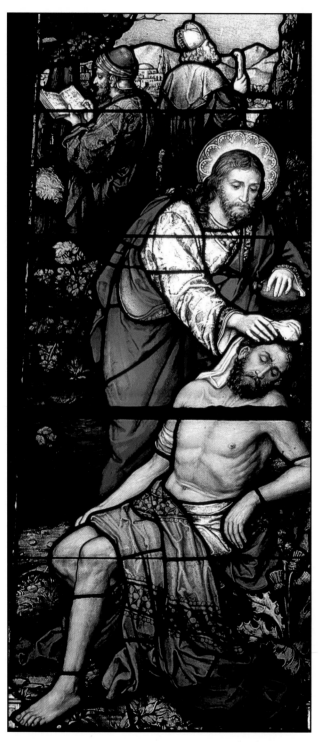

Good Samaritan,
Christ Episcopal,
St. Joseph,
Mayer of
Munich.

Opposite Page:
Wedding Feast at
Cana, Church of
the Risen Savior,
Rhineland, Frei
St. Louis &
Munich, 1920s.

In medieval and Renaissance Europe the physical and spiritual constantly interacted. It was a world of symbols and signs in the material world that told and foretold God's actions. If God is "the true light, which lighteth every man that cometh into the world," then the light that poured through the windows of the great cathedrals and small parish churches was symbolic of God's light. Abbot Suger, who designed the great Gothic church at the abbey of Saint-Denis in France at the beginning of the 12th century, wrote that churches could transform the material into the immaterial. "It seems to me that I see myself dwelling... in some strange region of the universe which neither exists entirely in the slime of earth nor entirely in the purity of Heaven; and that, by the grace of God, I can be transported from this inferior to that higher world."

St. Paul, Christ Episcopal, St. Joseph, Cox and Buckley, London and New York, c. 1886. The window is dedicated to Charles Franklin Robertson, the second Episcopal bishop of Missouri.

Opposite Page: Samaritan Woman at the Well, St. Henry Catholic, Charleston.

Annunciation, Grace and Holy Trinity Episcopal Cathedral, Kansas City, Powell/Whitefriars, 1930. Note the medieval use of colors and mosaic effect of the glass.

The Good Shepherd, Campus Lutheran, Columbia.

To move people to the spiritual realm was the goal of the great window designers. They relied on congregations to read the symbolic language of their work. Numbers, colors, shapes, even placement of the windows were symbolic. Lilies were a symbol of purity, palm leaves of martyrdom. St. Joseph, the father of Jesus, was recognized by his carpenter's tools, St. Mark, the evangelist, by the winged lion. Pairing New Testament scenes with Old was common. Selected scenes from the Old Testament were seen as predicting and paralleling events in the New Testament. For example, the story of Jonah emerging after three days in the belly of a whale might be placed opposite a window depicting the story of Jesus' resurrection.

St. Peter, St. Peter's Catholic, Jefferson City. Jesus holds the keys that are symbolic of Peter's leadership of the church. In the background is St. Peter's Basilica in Rome, a church not built for more than a thousand years after the scene depicted.

The origins of stained glass windows lie in the closing centuries of the Western Roman Empire. The earliest window glass was not clear, but colored with tints from impurities which could not be removed in the firing process. Earliest reports of colored glass being used in Christian churches date from the 4th century in Rome. These windows were filled with panes of different colored glass, "brilliant as the fields of flowers in Spring." At about the same time, in the eastern capital of Constantinople, religious iconography (the representation of religious subjects in pictures) developed around the construction of picture mosaics. The great Constantinople church, Hagia Sophia, "Holy Wisdom," built in the 6th century, had many mosaics covering its walls and domes. It was not a large step from setting small stones and bits of glass into patterns on a floor or wall to setting pieces of colored glass into similar patterns in windows.

Like much else in Western European culture, the art of stained glass traveled back with crusaders returning from the Holy Land. The oldest existing windows are in Augsburg, Germany (1065 CE), and Le Mans (1081 CE) and St. Denis (1108-1144 CE) in France. From the high quality of these windows we can conclude that they were not the earliest. Over the centuries technical processes, religious ideas, and artistic and architectural styles changed, leading to great changes in the windows produced.

Early glass makers wanted their windows to be easily understood by those who worshiped in the churches. The stained glass windows of the 12th century, the time of Abbot Suger of Saint-Denis, were characterized by rich colors and forceful geometric designs. The figures were large and made primarily of brightly colored glass, mostly reds, blues and greens, with little white or clear glass. These characteristics served the two purposes of stained glass: to provide radiance and beauty as a part of the total design of the church building and to teach Christian history and dogma in easily understood pictures.

These windows were not designed to provide realistic pictures. There was no attempt to put the scene into a spatial perspective. The pictures appeared completely flat and two-dimensional. Neither were the figures drawn to life-like proportions. They were often elongated to give them a superhuman grace, while the clothing was carefully depicted to show the folds in the garment of a stationary figure or the rippling clothes of a moving figure. Hands and feet were particularly elongated and curved. The folds of the clothing and curves of the bodies were highlighted by the placement of the lead lines, which outline the important elements in the picture.

Last Supper, Calvary Episcopal, Louisiana, Powell/Whitefriars, c. 1955-1960.

Opposite Page: *Grisaille* Windows, Ste. Genevieve Catholic, Ste. Genevieve, c. 1911.

Symbolism was used frequently to suggest elements of the story being told. A stone wall might indicate the complete building in which a saint stands, for example, or a single tree might represent a large forest. Colors were sometimes chosen that were different from realistic colors. Grass did not need to be green or the sky blue, if another color could be used to balance the others in the window or provide symbolic significance.

In the next century, ideas began to change and figures began to appear more realistic, mostly due to an increased use of painting to show additional details. This interest in detail began a gradual shift toward the artistic conventions that characterized the European Renaissance. Architectural discoveries in the 14th century allowed windows to become taller. These taller windows also became narrower with thinner stone traceries. At the same time, churches were becoming larger, requiring more light. In response to this need, craftsmen in France developed *grisaille* glass, clear or white glass delicately painted with black geometric and leaf patterns. More white glass was used also in figured windows, creating a lighter effect in keeping with the more delicate stone work. By the 15th century, windows had become mostly white glass with heavy use of Blessed James' new gold stain. Figures in windows became even more narrow to fit these new windows, and painting on even the stained glass became more important.

Medieval glass makers had not been interested in making realistic portraits of people, but of illustrating Christian doctrine and Bible stories. After the Renaissance began in the mid 14th century, artists became more interested in realism and the natural world. Figures became three-dimensional and were placed in more realistic three-dimensional settings. The portrayal of individual and natural beauty became more important than religious instruction. Gradually, Renaissance ideas took a firm hold and by the 16th century had replaced many medieval artistic concepts.

Painting became immensely important, so much so that designers wanted glass of more uniform thickness with fewer bubbles and ripples. The imperfections previously used to make the light more varied and brilliant were now considered undesirable. What was desirable was glass that would show the painting to the best effect. This trend reached its peak in the 17th and 18th centuries in Holland with the use of simple rectangles of white glass put together in a grid. On these panes of glass the artist would paint the entire picture, in much the same way an artist would paint on canvas. In these windows, there is no stained glass at all, merely a glass painting.

Lilies, Detail From Painted Annunciation, Visitation Catholic, Vienna, Ford, c. 1907.

Previous Page: To Feed the Hungry, From the Sequence The Corporal Works of Mercy, St. George Catholic, Hermann, Frei, 1926.

Born in Bethlehem.

Irwin

Nativity, Potosi Presbyterian, Potosi. The scene is painted rather than stained glass. Built in 1909, the church was designed in the English Gothic style by John Anderson Lankford, one of the first nationally prominent black architects. Lankford grew up in Potosi and was asked to design the church because of his ties to the congregation. The black dot above the horizon is a bullet hole.

Historians of stained glass generally agree that the quality of work declined from this time until the latter half of the 19th century. Most medieval skills and techniques were forgotten, and attempts to restore glass in need of repair were often done in ways that caused further damage. Changing artistic tastes in 18th and 19th century industrial England led to the replacement of many old windows by new ones thought to be more beautiful but generally considered to be unattractive today.

The history of European stained glass is not marred only by poor art. Serious destruction was done to windows at various times. During the reign of King Henry VIII of England, the motivation was individual greed and ambition. When he broke with the Catholic Church in the 16th century, Henry decided to break the power of the monasteries by dissolving them and confiscating their vast properties, destroying all their great churches in the process. In the next century, during the English Civil War, the religious intolerance of the Puritans and other sects led to the destruction of most of the remaining stained glass in English churches. In many English churches, Oliver Cromwell's religious zealots broke every pane of stained glass they could reach. In France a century later a combination of anti-religious sentiment and governmental greed prompted the sale of church art, including windows, to support Napoleon's wars.

In the last 150 years, however, serious craftsmen in Europe and America have recovered and improved upon the traditional techniques, giving us the beautiful stained glass in Missouri's churches. In England in the mid-1800s, craftsmen again became interested in stained glass. It was only one part of their interest in the medieval period generally. The industrial revolution was at full throttle, with huge economic and social consequences for the population. Many people were driven off the land in the largely rural country. Their labor was needed in factories being built in the cities, amassing huge fortunes for the owners but driving the workers into a level of destitution difficult for us to imagine. Starvation and disease killed thousands while a few became richer and richer. Instead of labor that was varied by the seasons and often done in community settings, factory labor was repetitive, unchanging and driven by the machine, not the cycles of the day or year. It is not surprising that scholars and ordinary persons alike would begin to yearn for a time when things were thought to have been simpler, when labor was done by hands not machines, and when ordinary people had beautiful things in their lives, even if they did not own them.

One man of supreme importance in the effort to regain a sense of human control and human dignity in the work of ordinary people was William Morris. A man of many talents, Morris designed stained glass windows, but he was also a poet and novelist, a political writer and organizer, as well as a designer of furniture, wallpaper, tapestries and other fabrics. He is said to have once remarked that a man who could not simultaneously weave a tapestry and compose an epic poem wasn't very talented. His interest in medieval work, art and life was enormous and his energy was boundless. He researched medieval ways of making stained glass and designing windows. Morris used the old formulas for making glass and employed medieval artistic concepts. In his work, the lead lines again became important to the curved and straight lines of figures, clothing and objects. Morris hired talented artists to do the basic drawings, which he then executed in stained glass. Although the 19th century saw a rejuvenation in stained glass art across Western Europe, many critics and art historians credit Morris with providing the leadership and inspiration in the effort to research and rediscover forgotten skills and knowledge, and to experiment with old and new techniques to achieve a level of craftsmanship missing since medieval times. It is ironic that today many English churches place little value on their wealth of late 19th century windows, thinking them far inferior to their remaining fragments of medieval glass.

Christians today have the Bible and other books to instruct them in their faith, and the purpose of stained glass has shifted away from instruction to the enhancement of the worship service. Modern designers can no longer count on church members' ability to read the symbolic language, and often resort to the use of words in windows to convey meaning to a more literate society. Many windows in Missouri churches are based upon the older traditions, however, and we may learn to understand the images with which they speak.

Opposite Page: Widow's Mite, Grace Episcopal, Jefferson City. Although there are few Morris windows in the United States and none known in Missouri, this figure is drawn in a style similar to that employed by Morris and his artists.

IN MEMORY OF
JULIA C. McCARTY
MAY 30th 1828. JAN. 25th 1895.

I Believe in the Holy Ghost, From the Sequence The Nicene Creed, Trinity Lutheran, Freistatt, Hopcroft, 1954.

Opposite Page: Presentation of Mary, St. Francis Borgia Catholic, Washington, Frei, c. 1905.

Resurrection, Immaculate Conception Catholic, Jefferson City.

Chapter 3
Religious &
Artistic Differences:
Stained Glass in America

I maintain that the best American colored windows
are superior to the best medieval windows.

— Louis Comfort Tiffany

B y comparison with the long rich tradition of stained glass
windows in Western Europe, America's tradition is both shorter
and, perhaps, less glorious. America was not discovered by
Europeans until near the end of the greatest period of stained glass
production. By the time Christopher Columbus brought the New World
to the attention of Europe, the medieval Christian faith, which had
inspired the beautiful windows of Europe's Gothic cathedrals and
churches, was waning. Both the Protestant Reformation and the more
secular artistic values of the Renaissance led to a decline in interest in
stained glass. These two momentous movements were to have an
important impact on the stained glass found today in churches around
the United States, and in Missouri.

Early American churches were usually simple in construction,
often made of wood, and were understood by even their builders to be
temporary structures. Consequently, cost considerations were often a
priority. Colored glass appeared in the windows of many colonial

American churches simply because it was cheaper and more readily available than clear glass. Much of the earliest stained glass used here was imported from Europe because it was more readily available there. The earliest record of glass production in North America is of Spanish craftsmen operating a glassworks in 1535 in Pueblo de los Angeles in Mexico. In the eastern colonies, there was little glass production until a century later.

The first stained glass maker along the east coast to leave a record was a Dutch immigrant named Everett Duycking in the colony of New Amsterdam, now New York. He came from Borken, now in Germany, in 1637 or 1638. There is a record of him taking on an apprentice in 1648, and at least one of his ten children also learned the craft. More Dutch and German glass makers came in the second half of the 17th century. So many came, in fact, that they opened enough other shops near Duycking's that in the 1650s the road was known as Glassmaker's Street. Skilled craftsmen continued to arrive through the early 1800s, settling in New Jersey and Philadelphia, and establishing successful companies. Some became quite large by the standards of that time. In 1769, for example, a Philadelphia glass shop owned by Heinrich Wilhelm Steigel employed 35 glass blowers and sold glass in all the major cities along the east coast.

In spite of the presence of this native industry, throughout the 18th century most stained glass used in American churches continued to be imported from Europe. Many of the colonial glassworks went bankrupt during the economic upheaval caused by the American Revolution, and Europe remained an important source of stained glass until well into the 19th century. In fact, stained glass from Europe continues to play an important role in the production of stained glass windows for American churches today.

Two occurrences contributed to an increased demand for stained glass windows in America in the middle of the 19th century. The first was a new wave of immigration from Western Europe, in particular from the Netherlands and Germany, beginning in the 1830s. A significant number of skilled craftsmen, including glass workers, were part of this influx of new Europeans. One critic of American stained glass commented cynically, "It now became possible to get a work of art in glass just as poorly made as if it had come from Europe." Some of these immigrants were to play an important role in the production of American stained glass. The second factor contributing to the increase was a boom in the building of churches. The 1840s saw the beginning of a revival of Gothic church architecture that significantly increased demand for stained glass windows.

Many of the Europeans who colonized North America belonged to Protestant religious denominations or sects that were indifferent, if not opposed, to stained glass windows in their churches. In fact, they often opposed church decoration of any kind. Early American church windows usually included no figures of saints or Gospel scenes. To those who practiced the austere religion of America's Puritans or similar sects, such things were papist (too closely associated with the Roman Catholic tradition) or idolatrous. These religious values have persisted in the United States and have had a profound impact on the number and kinds of windows found here. It has only been for the past century and a quarter that stained glass windows have become common in this country's churches. The first major installation of stained glass windows in a U.S. church was a joint project completed by French and New York firms in 1873 in St. John's in Washington, D.C.

An important American innovation in church windows came in the 19th century when John LaFarge popularized the use of opalescent glass for windows. Previously this glass was used for such items as pitchers, bowls and vases. Unlike the thin and brightly colored glass traditionally used in European churches, this glass was thick and the colors within a single piece of glass were streaked and marbled. As a result, much less light passed through the glass, making the colors far less brilliant. LaFarge was responsible, along with Louis Comfort Tiffany, for the subsequent boom in the production of opalescent glass, which reached significant levels by 1835.

Many Missouri churches now contain opalescent windows, including some designed by the Tiffany company. Opalescent glass found such widespread acceptance because it was considerably cheaper than traditional glass and required far less skill in design and fabrication. In addition, it provided colored light in churches which either opposed the use of religious art entirely or wanted to avoid seeming overly decorative. In Missouri churches it is most often found in windows with geometric patterns but no subject matter, in borders for figured scenes done in blown or cathedral glass, and in windows with medallions containing religious symbols. The first medallion window made in the United States was probably one made for First Presbyterian Church in Pittsburgh sometime between 1890 and 1908. It was not well received. The congregation disliked it so much that a large organ was placed in front of it so that it can now only be seen from the outside.

It was the use of opalescent glass for figured windows, however, which intrigued some American glass makers, including Louis Comfort Tiffany. Tiffany wanted to be able to create a figured window without the use of any painting, other than that required to provide facial and other flesh detail. He experimented with various ways to accomplish that, establishing his own glass factory in 1878 in order to maintain tighter control over the production. The method he favored involved forcing molten glass to wrinkle by compressing the partially cooled sheets. This wrinkling, Tiffany thought, worked to depict the folds in clothing without the use of paints and reduced the number of lead lines, which are used to create this effect in traditional stained glass. Although modern critics would disagree, Tiffany himself seemed in no doubt that he had been successful. He believed opalescent glass was in all ways superior. Another writer sharing Tiffany's view lamented the preference in Episcopal churches for traditional British stained glass over American

Star of David, Dove and Stone Tablets, Opalescent Medallions, United Hebrew, Joplin, 1916.

Previous Page: Iris, Detail From St. John the Evangelist, Trinity Episcopal, Hannibal, Tiffany.

Opalescent Figures, Detail of Presentation, Francis Street Methodist, St. Joseph, Ford, 1906.

Previous Page: Jesus Knocking at the Door, First Baptist, Kennett, c. 1905. The subject is taken from an English painting by William Holman Hunt, a pre-Raphaelite contemporary of William Morris. The painting is quite dark, with light only from the halo and a lantern in Jesus' hand. Windows of this subject typically include more light and dispense with the lantern. It is a common subject in Protestant church windows. The lack of an exterior latch on the door symbolizes the need for faith to open the door to Jesus' knock.

opalescent glass, writing, "There is no reasoning with sentiment. It affects our church architecture in general with a sameness and a tameness truly deplorable."

When opalescent glass was used for figured windows, it was frequently for so-called "landscape" windows. Landscape paintings have been immensely popular with Americans throughout our history, often playing on our emotional responses to our natural environment. For many churches whose members wished to have more decoration and art in their churches while avoiding the use of 'idolatrous" images, landscape windows were the answer. These windows could evoke sentimental responses from the viewer without presenting specific religious images that might be offensive in the particular denominational view. Sometimes landscape windows are said to be suggestive of religious ideas, but these are not usually readily apparent. Tiffany and other glass companies made hundreds of these windows for American churches, often copying a single artistic design for use in a number of churches. The "Hart" window by Tiffany found in Grace and Holy Trinity Cathedral in Kansas City is an example of such a window.

The trends in American stained glass that resulted from the development of opalescent glass in church windows took American churches far from the artistic and iconographic traditions of European stained glass. However, there were some in this country who sought to learn and employ medieval ideas and skills. Foremost among these was Charles Connick. He developed an interest in things medieval and in the late 1800s went to Europe to study stained glass. His experience in the great French cathedral of Chartres was life-changing. To say that he was captivated by the beauty of the medieval windows is an understatement. He remained in Paris for an extended period, unable to tear himself away. He returned to the cathedral day after day, studying the windows at different times of the day and in different weather, amazed by the play of light through the jewel-like glass of reds, blues and greens. He became convinced that only a strict adherence to medieval methods using the best mouth-blown glass could return the art of stained glass to the high position it had held in the 12th and 13th centuries. The studio he founded in Boston never deviated from his policy of using the finest glass. Connick refused to use opalescent glass because, he maintained, its milky quality detracted from the clarity of light, which was essential to the beauty of stained glass windows.

There were some elements of the American religious community that remained closer to those medieval European traditions than others, most notably the Episcopal and Roman Catholic churches. This is no

Hart, Grace and Holy Trinity Episcopal Cathedral, Kansas City, Tiffany, 1930. The window is a copy of a 1926 original destroyed in a fire in 1929. The inscription reads, "Like as the hart desireth the water brooks, so longeth my soul after thee, O God. To the glory of God and in memory of William Rockhill Nelson, Ida Houston Nelson, Laura Nelson Kirkwood."

surprise, since the religious and artistic traditions of the American branches of these churches were much more closely tied to the pre-Reformation Christianity that had inspired the great medieval windows than were American Protestant churches. Craftsmen who designed windows for Catholic churches, in particular, continued to work with the older iconography of New and Old Testament stories and the lives of saints, rendered in the more brightly colored, thinner translucent glass rather than opalescent glass. Much of Missouri's stained glass is the product of German immigrants who came to Missouri in the 1880s and 1890s and brought with them their own traditions, particularly the "Munich style" of highly ornamented windows influenced by German art and architecture of the Baroque period. These craftsmen created windows quite different in their artistic design from the work of

Mary and Jesus, Christ Church Episcopal Cathedral, St. Louis, Connick, 1928.

Opposite Page: Pieta, Shrine of Our Lady of Sorrows Catholic, Starkenburg, Frei, 1910.

Connick in Boston, but they used the mouth-blown glass they knew from their homeland. In Missouri Catholic churches built before World War II, they are the norm.

During the 20th century new stained glass workshops sprang up around the country. Some, like the Franz Mayer studio, which opened in Chicago in the early 1900s, were branches of European companies. Other major American studios included those of Connick in Boston, the Willet company in Philadelphia and the Frei company in St. Louis, which reversed the trend of European influence by opening and maintaining a workshop in Munich, Germany, for about thirty years. These companies met the demand for the more traditional style and iconography from the growing number of Catholic churches.

While stained glass windows are the product of a medieval world whose inhabitants would hardly recognize our own as related to theirs, the art of contemporary stained glass has been shaped by artistic and religious trends of our own day as strongly as medieval windows were by the values of that time. Ours is a more literate society, one in which most people have lost touch with the traditional iconography of the

Epiphany, St. Philip's Episcopal, Joplin, Ford, c. 1902.

Nativity, St. Thomas the Apostle Catholic, St. Thomas, Frei, 1920s.

Christian church. In addition, artistic values have undergone a revolution in this century, and that revolution can be seen in contemporary stained glass windows.

Medieval craftsmen thought of their work as utilitarian; the windows they designed for the great churches and cathedrals had particular functions. They served both architectural and religious purposes. The same is true of stained glass windows today. However, the art is quite different. Today's art is more abstract than that of the Tiffany or Munich style windows. Frequently windows have no subject matter at all. In other cases the subject matter is presented in very

St. John the Evangelist, Christ Episcopal, St. Joseph, Mayer of Munich.

Opposite Page: Wyd Was His Parisshe, Trinity Episcopal, St. James, Lamb, 1961. Located in New Jersey, Lamb is the oldest continuously operating stained glass studio in America.

The Last of Three Windows Depicting
the Story of Noah, St. Mary Catholic,
Cape Girardeau, 1950s.

abstract or impressionistic ways and is not readily apparent. Figures, when they do appear, seem two-dimensional or distorted in other ways, making them quite different from the three-dimensional figures and settings of the Munich style. The advent of newer construction materials has made very large windows possible, even walls made entirely of stained glass.

Virtually all the trends in American stained glass are represented in Missouri's churches. There are many windows of simple opalescent glass without any religious content, landscape windows, and medallion windows. There are also many excellent traditional stained and painted glass windows, as well as beautiful modern windows made from the very best mouth-blown glass.

Jesus Knocking at the Door, University Heights Baptist, Springfield.

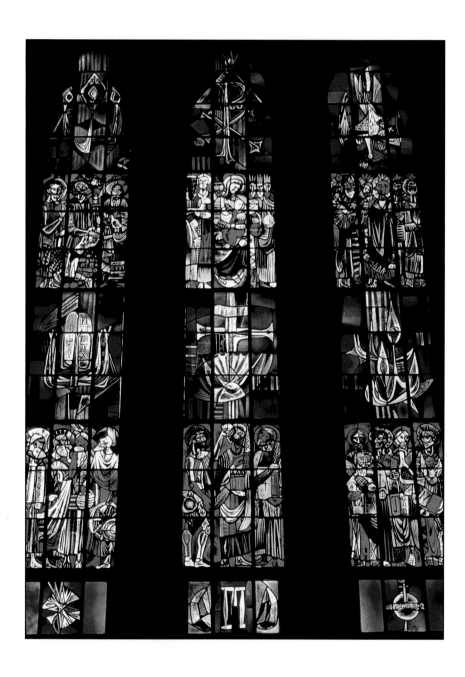

Trinity, St. Paul's Evangelical, Creve Coeur, Frei
(Designed by Rodney Winfield), 1961.

Chapter 4
A Vision of God's Paradise:
The Art of Missouri's Stained Glass

There is nothing ugly; I never saw an ugly thing
in my life: for let the form of an object be what it may,
— light, shade, and perspective will always make it beautiful.

— John Constable

Roger of Helmershausen was a monk who made religious art and taught his craft to others. In 1120, in his *Treatise of Divers Arts,* he quoted from Psalms, "Lord, I have loved the beauty of thine house." This passage could easily have been taken by the young men who were his pupils as their motto. It was their task to create windows for the new Gothic churches that would beautify and teach.

Sharing the sentiments of the Abbot Suger in France at the same time, Roger advised his students that those who designed beautiful windows would have

> shown forth to the beholders a vision of God's paradise, bright as springtide with flowers of every hue, fresh with green grass and flowers, refreshing the souls of the saints with crowns proportional to their divers merits, whereby thou makest the beholders to praise God in His creatures and to preach His wonders in His works... If he consider the light streaming through the windows, he marvelleth at the priceless beauty of the glass and at the variety of this most precious work.

"This most precious work" of God, the universe in which we humans live, should be brought to mind by the beauty of the stained glass. It would seem, then, that to truly appreciate stained glass windows we must learn to understand both the artistic beauty and the religious meaning of what we see. Only part of the work can be done by the artist; the rest we must do ourselves. American poet Nikki Giovanni wrote that a poem exists between the mind of the poet and the ear of the reader. We might just as accurately say that stained glass exists between the hand of the artist and the eye of the beholder. Beyond the simple judgment that something is beautiful because we happen to like it, how do we learn to appreciate stained glass?

The most important act in appreciating any kind of visual art, whether it is a painting, a statue or a stained glass window, is actually seeing it. We must learn to look carefully. We must also try to understand the particular artistic tradition in which the designer was working. Because artistic and religious traditions have changed dramatically over the centuries, it wouldn't be appropriate to judge a medieval or a Munich style window by the same criteria we use to comprehend a contemporary abstract window.

Missouri churches contain windows done in a wide range of artistic styles. Some follow the precepts of Charles Connick, using bright colors and containing multiple scenes within one large window. There are opalescent windows of all types and painted windows employing the approach of the 17th and 18th centuries. Particularly in Catholic churches, Munich style windows are prominent. In churches

Opposite Page: Resurrection, St. Paul's Episcopal, Kansas City, Jacoby, 1920s. Flowers and other natural elements are often a part of Munich style windows.

built since World War II, windows created in various modern artistic styles are common. Lest we be guilty of the same rash judgments as those Europeans who destroyed so many medieval and Renaissance windows because they had gone out of fashion, we need to judge each of these styles on its own merits, while keeping firmly in mind the purposes of stained glass windows in churches.

Modern windows can never exactly copy medieval windows. Neither we nor the designers of windows live in a medieval world. We can, however, judge whether a window uses colors appropriately within this tradition, for example, or whether the scenes within large windows follow the appropriate sequence.

In addition to windows produced by Connick, Jacoby, Frei and other American companies in the European tradition, Missouri has windows produced by European companies as well. Most prominent among the European companies represented in Missouri are Powell and Sons, also known as Whitefriars, of London, Mayer of Munich (which also had a studio in Chicago) and Tyrolean Art Glass of Innsbruck, Austria.

Historic Buildings, First Presbyterian, Cape Girardeau, Unique Art Glass.

Opposite Page: Jesus Preaching on Galilee, Unity Temple, Kansas City, Hopcroft (Designed by Paul Mann), 1971.

Others fell among the Thorns.

Fallen Among Thorns, From the Sequence The Parable of the Sower and the Seed, Zion Lutheran, Palmyra, 1914.

I Believe in the Holy Ghost, From the Sequence The Nicene Creed, St. Simon Cyrene Catholic (Formerly St. Philip Neri), St. Louis, Frei, 1932.

The American innovation of using opalescent glass to make church windows moved the craft in this country in an entirely opposite artistic direction. Opalescent glass is in some ways as far from traditional stained glass as was the painted glass of the 17th century. While the glass is certainly stained, it is almost entirely opaque (hence the term "opalescent"). As opposed to the very thin panes of blown glass, through which objects in the world outside the church can be discerned, opalescent glass does not allow one to see through it, no matter how strong the light. Few critics today have anything positive to say about opalescent glass windows. John Lloyd comments that art glass (another term used to describe this glass) has little art to it. If it is used to make "flat, solid, two dimensional effects [with] subdued color combinations and traditional leading techniques," it can serve the basic functions of a window. However, opalescent windows more typically follow the characteristics of Tiffany's work: "brilliantly colored scenes: highly realistic, artistic designs, and almost a fruity use of shape and color."

Dorcas, Second Presbyterian, Kansas City, Lamb, 1914.
This window is typical of the studio's earlier work.

Angel, Grace Episcopal, Jefferson City. The figure is taken from an Italian Renaissance painting by Fra Angelico.

In spite of the opinion of critics, opalescent glass has been highly popular in this country in part because it was less expensive than traditional glass, but also because it was used to create images that touched people's emotional and religious sensibilities. When used to create large brightly colored opalescent borders for narrative windows, the effects of direct sunlight can be quite dramatic. Most Missouri companies did at least some work in opalescent glass, and churches in the state also contain a great deal of opalescent glass by other American companies, most notably Tiffany and Ford. Opalescent windows have become associated in many minds with Victorian tastes and values, far too old fashioned for our more sophisticated modern world, and they are in danger of being relegated to the trash heap. They remain an important part of our history, however, a reminder of a time with religious and artistic values different from our own day, and the best of them deserve to be protected and preserved.

While the revival of medieval traditions provided one antidote to the American love of opalescent glass, German immigrants brought a completely different style window to this country. Munich style windows were made of blown glass and showed large, heroic figures under very highly decorated canopies of white and gold glass depicting stone arches and bordered by pillars made of the same glass. They are characterized most notably by this elaborate ornamentation, both in their borders and in the rendering of the pictures themselves. Highly skilled designers used the most translucent glass and deft paint strokes to create shimmering garments for their saints and angels. Architectural elements such as arches, columns and marble floors are presented in exquisite detail. There is an emphasis on contrasts between very bright and dark sections of the window as well as between contrasting colors, and there is a heavy reliance on painting to give added contrast between light and shadow. Figures are typically arranged in asymmetrical groups, with the two most important figures on the left, for example, with a group of five or six others on the right. This style was frequently used in Catholic churches in the first half of the 20th century.

More recently, trends in stained glass windows have reflected the changes in modern art. Pictures in windows have become less realistic, more abstract and more likely to employ symbols without using scenes or even figures. When they are used, figures are more likely to be two-dimensional and elongated with far less painting. Even details are rendered less realistically. In many ways, contemporary windows represent a return to medieval ideas. Both Rodney Winfield at Emil Frei

Associates and Robert Harmon have been strongly influenced by 12th century windows and medieval Greek mosaics. These artists do not simply copy a style, however, but use the earlier art as inspiration for their own very modern ideas. Contemporary windows must make concessions to our changing religious sensibilities. Our higher rates of literacy make it less necessary for windows to teach in the traditional sense. What they are more likely to do instead is to provide images on which we might focus our attention, and about which we might meditate. Stephen Frei, head of Emil Frei Associates and great-grandson of the company's founder, comments that he wants a person to return to a contemporary Frei window again and again, each time noticing something new.

Annunciation, St. Vincent de Paul Catholic, Cape Girardeau, c. 1986. This photograph shows how what is outside can affect what someone inside sees. The splash of red in the bottom is from a car parked nearby. Cars moving past the window, and even the passing of seasons, constantly change the appearance of a window.

Holy Family, Twin Spires Museum (Formerly Immaculate Conception Catholic), St. Joseph, Frei, 1908.

St. Paul Escaping in a Basket, St. Paul's Evangelical, Creve Coeur,
Frei (Designed by Rodney Winfield), 1961.

Two other styles must be mentioned—etched glass and faceted glass. Etched glass is formed by cutting a pattern on clear or lightly colored glass with a fine stream of sand particles blasted at the glass. In appearance, etched glass is reminiscent of medieval *grisaille* windows, made with clear or white glass on which a pattern was painted using black or brown paint in geometric or leaf patterns. Similar to etched glass, sculpted glass is made using the same technique but with heavier, deeper cuts. Rarely used for figures, etched and sculpted glass are often used in wooden, colonial type churches in which figured stained glass would seem inappropriate.

Faceted glass is a thick, molded glass that produces much different effects than other types of glass. Because of its thickness, it requires thicker support than the lead used in other windows. Consequently, a faceted glass window has relatively more dark spaces, reducing the amount of light that passes through. It is not typically used in small pieces in intricate designs, but in larger pieces. It can be used to form relatively simple but effective figured windows with a limited number of carefully chosen colors. It is perhaps most effective in large symbolic or abstract designs which allow more light to pass through. Faceted glass can create a moving effect in modern buildings.

While individual tastes differ, one can learn to judge windows on how well they accomplish the functions of stained glass windows and to appreciate them within their own artistic traditions. Done well, a stained glass window adds to the beauty and spirituality of the church building. Done poorly, it can distract, annoy and interfere with the religious activities taking place within that space.

Visiting the Imprisoned, From the Sequence of Corporal Works of Mercy, St. Cecelia Catholic, Kennett. Here faceted glass is used in very limited colors quite effectively to illustrate the spiritual quality of the act by portraying the light entering through the prison bars.

St. Peter and St. Andrew, Grace Episcopal, Carthage.

St. Ludger and St. Boniface, St. Joseph Catholic, Westphalia, Frei, 1905. Ludger (left) is shown holding a church, symbolic of the churches he founded. Boniface holds a palm symbolic of his martyrdom.

Chapter 5

Light into Darkness:
Iconography

In the beginning was the Word,
and the Word was with God,
and the Word was God ...
In him was life;
and the life was the light of men.
And the light shineth in the darkness;
and the darkness comprehended it not.

— John 1:1, 4-5

In the medieval world, light was understood to be the symbol of creation, of the divine light of wisdom and revelation (God's greatest gifts to humanity) and of the presence of God in the world. Medieval Christian mystics often described their experience of God's presence as the apprehension of pure light. Missouri stained glass designer Robert Harmon explained his approach in similar language. God is pure light, he said, but humans are not able to perceive pure light. In the ordinary world we perceive things because they reflect part of the light shed on them. Harmon said his task in designing a stained glass window was to bring the pure light of the spirit into the holy spaces set aside for worship by fracturing that pure light into colors that the human eye can recognize. Thus, on one level, the purpose of a stained glass window is to make God visible to the human eye. Although we can never comprehend God completely, we can approach God in steps, through the reds, blues, greens and golds of a window. This can be done by a window with no subject matter at all, but the presence of a subject can provide an additional means of focusing a person's attention on spiritual matters.

Virtually all traditional church architecture carries with it some spiritual symbolism. For example, the long, narrow main section of a traditional church building is called the nave, from *navis,* the Latin word for ship. In Christian thinking, the church is the means to salvation replacing Noah's ark—the Old Testament ship that saved mankind from the destruction of the Flood. From the medieval period on, however, stained glass windows have carried much of the most obvious symbolism within the church. One major purpose of medieval windows was to instruct Christians in their faith. In a time when few Europeans could read, the windows carried important lessons to the vast majority of Christians. Abbot Suger wrote, "The pictures in the windows are there for the sole purpose of showing simple people who cannot read the Holy Scriptures what they must believe." A 12th century catechism, a book of religious instruction, asked, "What should one do on entering a church? One should take Holy Water, adore the Blessed Sacrament and then walk round the church and contemplate the windows."

Nativity, St. Joseph Catholic, Louisiana. Note the medieval-style use of internal light coming from the infant to illuminate the scene.

Opposite Page: Crucifixion, Visitation Catholic, Vienna, Ford, 1907. The designer of this window used a small amount of stained glass for the figures while relying on painted clear glass to create a dramatic lighting effect.

Mary Crowned
Queen of Heaven,
St. Andrew
Catholic, Tipton.

Opposite Page:
Last Supper, Unity
Temple, Kansas
City, Hopcroft
(Designed by Paul
Mann), 1971.

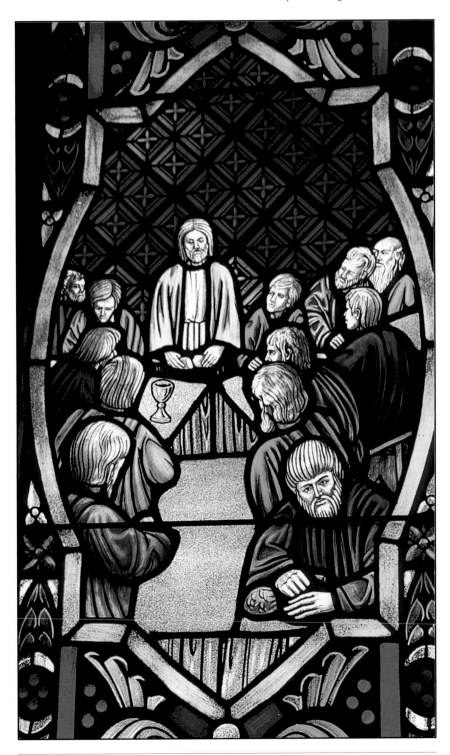

Because of the stress placed on the lessons of the windows, medieval Christians were probably much more knowledgeable about the meaning of the figures and symbols than contemporary Christians. Lawrence Lee, a modern day expert on stained glass windows, comments that the medieval peasant might be amazed at the glorious colors of the new windows in the church, because his was a world of natural light generally lacking in artificially colored light. He would have been much more familiar with the images in the windows, the saints and scenes from the life of Christ and the saints.

A modern viewer, used to artificial light, is much more likely to take for granted the brightness of the colors but be puzzled by the images. In the more literate world of today, we are apt to require a written explanation of the meaning of the windows because we do not possess a familiarity with Christian symbolism. We do not understand Christian iconography as it is represented in stained glass windows made today or five centuries ago. We may not even know the meaning of the word "iconography." We do not know how to "read" a window. Where do we begin?

Pelican, Detail from Mary and Jesus Window, Christ Episcopal Cathedral, St. Louis, Connick, 1928. There was a widely held medieval belief that when a pelican could not find other food, it would peck its breast and allow the drops of blood to fall into the beaks of its young. Thus, it became a common symbol of Jesus' sacrifice of his blood for humanity. Missouri has several church windows depicting pelicans.

Opposite Page: Annunciation, St. Francis Borgia Catholic, Washington, Frei, c. 1905.

Iconography is the entire set of traditional symbolic forms associated with a subject and the conventions that define those forms and determine how they are used in relation to each other. These forms and conventions include many things we would not generally associate with spiritual meaning. For example, in traditional church architecture and the placement of windows, even compass directions had meaning. North represented the past, and any windows containing Old Testament subjects were placed on that side of the church. South represented the present, so New Testament windows were placed on the south side of the nave. In many churches, including Missouri United Methodist in Columbia, windows were designed to follow a typological iconography. For example, a north window including symbols of creation from Genesis is opposite a south window with symbols of the nativity of Jesus; another north window showing Moses and the four major prophets of the Old Testament is opposite a window of Christ and the four evangelists. Direction is important in another sense as well. Just as with a printed page, a complex stained glass window with many sections is normally read left to right but bottom to top.

Colors also carry many symbolic meanings and are used according to certain conventions. Blue is symbolic of spiritual love, constancy and fidelity, so it is no surprise that Mary, the mother of Jesus, is usually shown wearing a blue cloak. Often her robe is white, the color of purity, and she is frequently shown with a vase of white lilies. Red may be the symbol of blood and suffering, while green is symbolic of hope. The symbolic meaning of colors is not as simple as this sounds, however. While yellow or gold is symbolic of the sun, and hence the Son of God, it can also represent deceit, jealousy, cowardice or treason.

The symbolism related to numbers and shapes is as complex and baffling as that of colors. The number "1" suggests the unity of God; the number "2" symbolizes dualities such as good and evil, light and darkness or time and eternity. The Trinity is represented by "3" and, by extension, the triangle because of its three sides. Because of the stability of the triangle (a three-legged stool is more stable than a four-legged chair, for example) "3" also came to represent stability. Because God is the only perfect being, the shape made by a single line, the circle, came to represent God and the idea of perfection. Like God it has no beginning and no end and is without irregularities.

Opposite Page: Creation, St. Charles Borromeo Catholic, St. Charles, Frei, 1950s.

Many of the windows in Missouri churches make use of this traditional iconography. It can often be seen at its most obvious in the depictions of saints. The simple halo, or circle of light, surrounding the head of a saint has many symbolic implications. It indicates the holiness of the person because it is a visual expression of supernatural light, a spiritual crown bestowed in recognition of the saint's achievements in the struggle with evil. The word "halo" derives from the Greek word that means sun, indicating its close connection with light. The traditional shape of the halo is circular, indicating the perfection achieved through salvation.

Individual saints are traditionally shown in particular ways, allowing us to identify them even when the saint's name does not appear in the window. If we see a man depicted with a halo, long beard and a set of keys, for example, it must be Peter. If the man is bald with a beard and holding a sword with its point resting on the ground, it is likely to be Paul. The man with the book, quill pen and ox is the evangelist Luke.

Gethsemane, First Christian, Carthage. Some Protestant churches were opposed to showing halos, but the artist here creates a halo effect with light without actually including one.

St. Cecelia, Immaculate Conception Catholic, New Madrid. Windows of St. Cecelia, patron of music, are frequently placed in choir lofts.

The specific images used with other saints may be more obscure, but they often point us to interesting stories told about the saint's life. Gertrude is a less well-known saint than Peter or Paul, but sometimes included in Catholic churches, particularly in German communities. She is usually shown holding a tall staff, on which a mouse is crawling towards her hand. Gertrude lived in a convent in the 7th century. She was especially known for her patience, and it is said that the devil tested her by taking the form of a mouse and gnawing through yarn that she was spinning. In response to the prayers of peasants in 1822 in the lower Rhine valley in western Germany and Belgium, she is credited with saving the crops from a plague of mice and rats. Apparently, at least some of the German peasants who emigrated from this area to rural Missouri in the 1800s brought their devotion to St. Gertrude with them.

The images in the windows of some saints are more macabre. For example, St. Lawrence is usually pictured with a large gridiron, or grill. It is said that he angered the rulers of 3rd century Rome by giving the church's wealth to the poor in order to keep city officials from confiscating it. As a punishment, he was condemned to be roasted over a slow fire. Lawrence is said to have borne his suffering patiently, even maintaining his sense of humor, telling those torturing him to turn him over because he was done on one side. Perhaps it is in keeping with this sense of humor that Lawrence later became the patron saint of cooks and is invoked for protection against fire.

While we are not likely to find any saint other than Peter depicted with keys, there are some symbols used with many saints. Lilies are a symbol of purity and are often included in depictions of Mary, Joseph and other saints who were virgins. Saints appearing with palm leaves were martyred for their faith. Men who were bishops typically wear the bishop's tall, peaked hat, called a miter, and hold a crooked staff, symbol of the bishop's role as shepherd of the faithful. Saints holding a model of a church building were individuals who founded churches, monasteries or convents.

Previous Page: St. Peter, Benedictine Chapel of Perpetual Adoration, Clyde, Tyrolean Art Glass, 1900-1912.

Opposite Page: St. Gertrude, Sacred Heart Catholic, Rich Fountain, Frei, 1920s. When viewing the window in person, be sure to look for the blue mouse crawling up the bottom of her staff.

Nativity, St. John Nepomuk, St. Louis, Frei Munich studios, 1929.

Armed with this introduction to Christian iconography, we can apply what we have learned to a stained glass window from a Missouri church. Perhaps the first thing to notice about the window from St. John Nepomuk is that it compresses two Biblical stories into one narrative window. It presents us with images typical of a window showing the birth of Jesus, but also includes the story of Epiphany, the visit of the Magi. It is as though the shepherds and the three kings have arrived simultaneously. We see one shepherd and one wise man kneeling, while the other two magi and three shepherds stand looking on. The other figures in the scene are an angel, presumably one of those announcing the birth to the shepherds, and the dove representing the Holy Spirit. There are two lambs included. One being carried on the shoulders of a young shepherd suggests the parable of the Good Shepherd, while the one lying on the ground hints at Jesus as the sacrificial lamb who will give up his life. The magi hold the gifts they have brought, and the one who is kneeling has laid aside his crown. Placed at the foot of the manger in which the infant lies, it symbolizes the future kingship that awaits him.

In addition to the figures themselves, there are several traditional uses of iconography. Most of the figures have halos; only the shepherds do not. Mary is dressed in blue, while the three kings wear royal colors: reds, golds and purples. The use of light is one of the most striking symbolic elements. In a relatively dark window, light radiates through the figure of the infant in the manger—Jesus portrayed as the Light of the World.

As with medieval windows, this window requires enough basic knowledge of the story to identify it. Beyond that, one needs to "read" the window and, as we know, learning to read requires practice.

Phoenix, Detail from Resurrection window, Westminster Presbyterian, St. Joseph, Willet, 1963. The phoenix is a symbol of resurrection.

Resurrection, Happy Zion
General Baptist, Annapolis,
Harmon, 1999. Notice the
dogwood and daffodil
blossoms, drawn from
Harmon's—and the
church's—surroundings.

A Journey through Light:
In Memory of Robert Harmon

I saw Eternity the other night
Like a great ring of pure and endless light.

— "The World," Henry Vaughan

As an artist, Robert Harmon had little interest in paint and even less in canvas. Harmon worked with light. It was both his material and his message.

Harmon was a student in his mid-twenties at the School of Fine Arts at Washington University in St. Louis when Emil Frei Jr. chose him to come to work at the Frei stained glass company in the city. Harmon had grown up in a religious family; his father was a minister in the Christian church and an excellent Biblical scholar. His background in religion had not taught him much about Christian iconography, however, and he set out on a life-long study of the symbols of the Christian faith.

Emil Frei Jr. was interested in moving away from the Munich style windows that had characterized his father's era as head of the company. Harmon's own artistic ideas, based on his interest in and knowledge of modern abstract art in its various styles, meshed naturally into Frei's plans for a new direction for the firm. He never cared all that much about subject matter as an important element in his work, he said. "I can do without it, or I can work with it." What Harmon helped Frei do was to was to move the company into window design that was revolutionary, that turned away from the old principles of realistic or idealistic portrayals of people and scenes. Harmon and the younger Frei wanted to get at the essence of the religious experience and depict it in such a way that people were challenged to think and to constantly look at the windows anew.

Harmon's career spanned six decades. He made windows for five cathedrals and innumerable churches in the United States. For more than twenty years, he worked independently out of his own studio in rural Missouri. His inspiration came not only from his religious faith and the traditions of religious art, but also from his Ozark environment. Harmon said the essential elements in his creative world included the things around him: the valley, the rocks, and the water. Water is particularly important. In his windows, light takes on a liquid quality. Light flows like water.

Harmon is regarded as one of the premier designers of stained glass windows in the United States during the last half-century. His reputation was built primarily on his design of massive windows. Sometimes creating a virtual wall of stained glass of immense proportions, his windows are thin membranes barely separating the quiet, sacred space within from the bustling, noisy world without. But, as he pointed out, that world outside is also lit by the Light of the World.

Robert Harmon
in his Missouri
studio, 1999.

Detail from Christ the Man of Sorrows, St. Mark's Episcopal, St. Louis, Frei (Designed by Robert Harmon), 1938. The windows of St. Mark's comment on war and other problems of the day.

Angel, Detail of Annunciation, St. Joseph Catholic, Kimmswick.

Chapter 6
Turning Sand into Light:
The Production Process

Light (God's eldest daughter)
is a principal beauty in building.

— The Holy State and the Profane State, Thomas Fuller

Standing in front of a stained glass window through which the sun is throwing golden and red light into the church interior, it is hard to remember that glass is essentially melted sand. The transformation of this heavy, earth-bound substance into the heavenly light of a stained glass window seems a miracle in itself.

A stained glass window is built of a multitude of pieces of white and colored glass held together by leading, grooved strips of lead soldered at the joints. The colors can be arranged in such a way as to form a picture, with the robe of Jesus consisting of pieces of white glass, the garment of John the Baptist made of brown, the Jordan River done in blue, and so on. When the artist wants to add details, such as the folds in a robe or waves on water, he carefully adds black or brown enamel paint in delicate lines or soft brush strokes. The painting of faces requires particular care and skill to achieve the desired effect. The painted piece of glass is then fired in a kiln to fuse the paint to the glass.

Humans have been making glass for thousands of years. We don't know how the discovery was made, but the Roman writer Pliny tells one interesting story. In the ancient world, sailors in the Mediterranean Sea never intentionally got out of sight of the land and came to shore each evening. Pliny reports that Phoenician sailors went ashore one evening and built fires on the sand to cook their meal. Unable to find anything lying nearby on which to rest their cooking pots, they went to their ship to get blocks of niter (sodium bisulphate), a substance commonly used on ancient ships. When these blocks were heated sufficiently by the sailors' cook fires, the sodium bisulphate combined with the heated sand to create a crude form of glass.

Early glass manufacturing involved melting a mixture of sand and potash or soda in heat resistant tubs. Theophilus, a monk in an 11th century German monastery, gave this recipe for glass: two parts ashes from beech wood or bracken, one part river sand and a little sea salt. Old methods of glass manufacture produced glass with impurities which affected the color and left air bubbles and lines in the sheets of glass. Today's techniques are more refined, and modern glass can be made with virtually no flaws such as air bubbles or scars. For stained glass windows, however, those imperfections are important elements in creating the beauty of the windows as the light passing through the glass is bent and fragmented by the changes in density.

There are two traditional ways of shaping molten glass into the finished product. One is to pick up a small amount of the molten liquid on the end of a hollow tube through which the glass maker blows to form a bubble called a muff. The muff is enlarged through the addition of more air and by turning the bubble. As it begins to cool it is cut open and carefully flattened to form a disk. The other method is to simply spin the mass of molten glass on the end of a stick until it forms a disk of cooling glass. Using these methods, skilled craftsmen can produce pieces of glass only 1/8 of an inch thick. In general, the thinner the glass, the more effectively it transmits light. These traditional methods still produce the finest glass used in windows, so thin and pure that you can easily see through even pieces of dark color. But today glass is also produced in large quantities by methods developed during the industrial revolution. These methods usually involve molten glass being poured into molds or rolled flat by large industrial rollers.

Color is added at the time the glass is molten. Medieval glass makers had a more limited range of colors available than today's designers. Their colors depended on the materials available as additives. An oxide of cobalt from Bohemia produced blue glass; manganese was added to this mixture for violet; copper oxide for blue-green. Red was produced by a mixture of oxidized copper and iron. A bioxide of copper created green, to which cobalt could be added for a blue tint. Yellow glass, the discovery attributed to Blessed James, was made possible by the addition of ferrous oxide and manganese. This was the full range of colors available to the medieval glass maker. Today, virtually any shade of any color can be produced, from traditional hues to exotic pastel pinks or muted grays.

Today's stained glass window designer has a variety of glass types available. In addition to the traditional blown glass used for centuries, there is the similar cathedral glass produced by the modern industrial methods described above. Flashed glass involves fusing a sheet of thin colored glass onto another sheet of glass which is clear or another color. Faceted glass is a much thicker glass formed by pouring the molten glass into molds and allowing it to cool. When it is used in windows it is typically chipped on the interior side to cause the light passing through to be refracted. Of course, many American window designers have also favored opalescent glass.

Once the glass has been manufactured, colors are selected and sheets cut to fit a pattern drawn by the artist for a particular window. Usually subjects for windows are suggested by the leadership of the particular church and then worked by the artist to meet the demands of religious doctrine, architectural structure and budget. Louis Comfort Tiffany described the process of creating a stained glass window at the beginning of the 20th century. It was a process very similar to the one employed by the medieval craftsman 800 years earlier. Today the use of computers has modified the process in some firms, but Tiffany's description, reprinted below, still provides us with a basic understanding. Once decisions have been made regarding the basic elements such as subject, glass type, window size and placement, the designer begins by creating drawings.

A color sketch for composition and the distribution of colors leads to the grand cartoon [a window-sized drawing of the sketch]. From this, two transfers are made on paper. One is kept as a guide for the artist who arranges the leads and puts the glass pieces together. The other is divided on the lines for the leads, being cut into separate patterns which are arranged on a glass easel; this is placed against a strong light. The patterns are easily removable. Selecting the sheet of glass which seems to hit the right color for the given section of the design, the artist removes the paper pattern at that point from the easel and passes the sheet of colored glass between his eyes and the opening left by the pattern he has removed. Marking that part of the colored sheet which has been selected, the glassman then places the paper pattern upon it and cuts round its edges with a diamond. The piece thus shaped is then fixed with wax to the glass easel whence the paper pattern has come. Thus, piece by piece, glass in various colors and shades takes the place of the paper. Changes are often made.

In general, each time an artist wants to change colors, he must choose another piece of glass. One exception to this rule is the use of the silver oxide of Blessed James to stain white glass yellow. In this way, the face of a saint and the golden halo do not need to be from separate pieces of glass. Elaborately designed figured windows can consist of hundreds or even thousands of pieces of glass. The scale of some windows is staggering. The great east window in York Minster in England, for example, measures 72 x 32 feet, roughly the size of a tennis court. In Chartres Cathedral in France, there were originally 185 figured windows that included more than 8,000 separate figures and over 2,000 square meters of glass. With an average piece of glass being only a few square inches, how many pieces of glass might there be in such a church? One million? Two? Missouri churches also have such elaborately designed windows. In the Presentation window done by Powell for Grace and Holy Trinity Episcopal Cathedral in Kansas City, for example, one square foot of the window contains more than one hundred pieces of glass.

The process of selecting colors is a complex one. The designer must judge the appearance of each colored pane of glass by itself, as Tiffany suggests. He must understand the ways in which panes of different colors of glass will transmit light. Colors do not respond in the same ways to the light passing through them. Blue becomes a dominant color in a window, especially on dark overcast days. Red is a rich color, but a pane of red glass of ordinary thickness can appear almost black, so that red glass must be made particularly thin, too thin to resist the ordinary stresses on window glass. Consequently, the red glass is then "flashed," heat-bonded onto a thicker clear sheet of glass to strengthen it. Large amounts of any one color will produce effects quite unlike small amounts of the same color. Colors look different depending on the colors they are near. Red adjacent to blue provides effects quite distinct from red alongside white. In addition, there is the need to consider the religious implications of the colors.

Glass can be cut in complicated shapes in order to show details in the window, the curve of Jesus' elbow beneath his robe, for example. The dark line of lead which joins the pieces of glass outlines the design and makes the picture easier to see. In a well-made window, there will

Presentation, Grace and Holy Trinity Episcopal Cathedral, Kansas City,
Powell/Whitefriars of London, 1930.

Servants, Detail of Wedding Feast at Cana, Church of the Risen Savior
Catholic, Rhineland, Frei, c. 1920s.

be few lead strips that do not follow the natural pattern of the picture. Poorly designed windows will often have large pieces of glass set in lead strips that do not highlight the shapes of the images in the window.

Depending on the type of glass used and the design called for, after the glass is cut it may be painted on one or both sides and fired in a kiln to bond the paints to the glass. Pieces of glass are then placed together according to the pattern, using lead strips to hold them in place. Sections of the window are assembled in the workshop and then transported to the site, where they are installed into the openings to form the entire window.

Although the description of the process of making a stained glass window may sound as though it is a craft with the object of producing a material product, we need to remember that for most members of this craft throughout history, it has been a labor done as much with an eye on the spiritual world as on this one. Lawrence Lee wrote about the men and women who design these beautiful windows, "The fact that some entrancing details... are often found in high traceries where only binoculars can bring them to a size sufficient for full appreciation is surely a sign that the artist knew himself to be engaged on work whose sanction was more than public approbation."

The best stained glass windows are works of art, and as William Morris, who created so many beautiful windows in his life, said, "Art is the expression by man of his pleasure in labour." As you look at stained glass windows, remember to search for those entrancing details—those expressions of pleasure.

Trademark of Powell/Whitefriars, Detail of Tree of Life, Trinity Episcopal, St. James, 1930. Powell often used only the figure of the monk as its trademark, without the company name. Trademarks are uncommon, making identification of the company very difficult.

Presentation, Francis Street Methodist, St. Joseph, Ford, 1906.

Chapter 7
Donors & Artists:
An Example from Francis Street Methodist

She has done what she could. Easter 1885.

— Memorial window inscription, Christ Episcopal Church, St. Joseph

Throughout history, artists have been supported by donors or patrons, those who commissioned works of art and paid for them once they were produced. Those great artists whose names are unknown today but who crafted the beautiful religious art of medieval Europe were supported by the churches which they decorated. The great Italian Renaissance artists, Michelangelo, Raphael, Leonardo and others were supported by the church or by wealthy patrons. Those artists who have worked in stained glass throughout the centuries have been no different. Their work has been made possible by the families and individuals who donated money to the churches to pay for the windows.

Churches recognize the important role played by these donors. Even when churches remember little else about their stained glass windows, they hold onto the knowledge of the donor's identity. Churches generally considered the identity of the artists that created the windows to be unimportant, and the companies that made many beautiful windows are often forgotten today by those who admire and benefit from their work each Sunday. However, the names of the donor families are often included in the windows for all to see and remember.

Who were these families and individuals, and what was their role in the creation of these works of art? In some instances, donors simply provided money to pay for windows. In others, the donors played a role in the design of the windows. An example of the latter is found in the records of the Francis Street Methodist Church in St. Joseph. In 1905 the congregation was constructing a new church. Several families wished to contribute to the building by donating stained glass windows. At least one of those families, the Hoaglands, was represented on the building committee. Theodore Hoagland played a very assertive role in the process. On March 31, 1905, he wrote to the New York architect:

> We have settled upon the "Nunc Dimittis" which of course is the scene in the temple when Simeon is blessing the Infant Christ by Fra Bartolommeo. There is another painting of the same incident by another of the old masters but we prefer this one. However we will want the picture of the Virgin made more youthful looking and also the picture of Joseph, while the Prophetess Anna should look more like an old woman. Her garb also should not be that of a nun as shown in the original. With these changes the picture will be all right.

The family was interested in correcting what it saw as inaccuracies in the painting that was to serve as a model for the window. The inclusion of a figure in a nun's habit was not acceptable in the Protestant church. Hoagland and his mother, who was providing the money, had other suggestions which he included in the same letter.

> My Father was a very patient man and if you choose to weave any part of his character into the picture it might be patience. Text "In your patience possess ye your souls," or "Let Patience have her perfect work." When asked how he was he almost always said, "I am waiting." These three words might be brought in somehow. We think of the above Scripture passages, that the [second] "Let Patience have her perfect work," is the better.

In later letters, it became clear that these were more than suggestions. The Hoaglands saw them as requirements. In a May 30th letter to the architect, Hoagland rejected the plans proposed by the Tiffany company because the drawings did not include the texts.

In responding to drawings provided by the Ford Brothers Glass Co. of Minneapolis, the company which eventually provided the windows, he voiced several objections.

> It is his [the pastor's] opinion and the opinion of all who have examined the design which you presented, that the picture is too small, embracing only the center panel and that it should embrace two more panels, one on either side of the center panel, thus taking in more figures of the

Borremio [sic] painting. It is also the opinion that the inscription, I Am Waiting, should be either on or below the first pannel [sic] and that the inscription, "Let Patience Have Her Perfect Work," should be either on or below the last panel.

The Ford company was willing to make the desired changes and in August 1905 received the contract to provide all the stained glass windows for the church. The Hoagland memorial window cost $2,000. The contract allowed Mrs. Hoagland to make changes she desired in the decorative glass surrounding the picture, and not to pay for the window until it was to her "entire satisfaction." Given this last stipulation, we can assume the company was most eager to complete the project, especially after receiving the following information from Hoagland in June 1906:

I am very anxious to know just when you can ship the balance of this work, as my mother, who is placing the memorial window for my father, is over 90 years old and quite feeble and was quite sick a few weeks ago, and we feared she would drop off before this window was placed and she has set her heart on seeing it before she goes.

In the same June letter, Hoagland told the company of the response to the installation of some of the smaller windows of opalescent glass.

Every one who has seen the work which you have already furnished for the Church think [sic] the windows are beautiful and give a very pleasing effect, some people however think they are a little dark, that is that they will not transmit light, though I think probably this is a mistake and so thinks our Minister.

Several weeks later, days after the installation of other windows showing the Good Shepherd, Jesus in the house of Mary and Martha, and Jesus knocking at the door, he informed Ford, "I take pleasure in saying that, so far, I have not heard an unfavorable comment or criticism of the work." He again commented that his mother "is of course very anxious" to see the memorial window completed, "as I presume it will be the first of next week."

The work was completed, and on July 24th he wrote to the company, "My mother was at the church this morning and inspected the memorial window. She was greatly pleased with it." Ford Brothers was paid for its work, and today the congregation is proud of its windows.

Last Supper, First Christian, Independence, Hopcroft, c. 1997.

Chapter 8

Through Good Times & Bad:
Missouri Stained Glass Companies

Bright is the noble edifice that is pervaded by the new light.

— On His Church of St. Denis, Abbot Suger

Evidence of stained glass work in Missouri dates to a directory of St. Louis businesses for 1857. Two entries, for "Farmer and Son" and for "Miller and Boisaubin (importers and manufacturers)," appear under the listing for "Glass Stainers." A Missouri business directory for 1860 includes Bierworth, the first German name in a long line of German immigrant workers in stained glass in St. Louis. This same directory includes a listing for a St. Joseph "painter and glazier," but it is doubtful this company's work included stained glass.

In fact, we have no way of knowing what kind of windows any of these firms produced. If any remain in existence, they are unknown today. This is also true for companies in business in the later 19th and early 20th centuries. Much of the work of the early Missouri companies which designed stained glass windows went into private homes rather than public buildings. Often these windows were not stained glass, but were clear glass decorated by etching or beveling. In some instances, examples of residential stained glass produced by some of these companies exist, but there is no identified work in churches. It may be that the firms worked only in residential windows or that their work in churches has been destroyed or cannot be identified.

According to the 1890 national Census of Manufactures, Missouri had fourteen companies working in "obscured glass, including cathedral and skylight." Surely many, if not all, of these companies worked entirely in windows for residential use. Research for this book has not found any church window verifiably produced by a Missouri company prior to 1900. The 1900 Census of Manufactures counted seventeen Missouri companies in the category of "glass-cutting, staining and ornamenting." This number seems to have been relatively consistent over the next several decades.

How does Missouri compare to other states in the production of these kinds of windows? In 1890, Missouri ranked fifth behind New York, Pennsylvania, Illinois and Massachusetts. In 1900, Missouri was fourth, having surpassed Massachusetts. In spite of its high ranking, Missouri produced only a fraction of what was produced in New York and Pennsylvania. For example, in 1900 Missouri produced a total value of "obscured glass" equal to only one-fourth of New York's production. By 1910, New York was producing ten times as much as Missouri, and Pennsylvania almost eight times as much.

Many companies offered other types of windows or services. Several handled ornamental windows, but also sold ordinary glass and large plate glass windows. Some were essentially interior decorating companies that included ornamental glass among their products. Only a few specialized in stained glass and even fewer in church windows. From the work remaining in Missouri churches, we can identify a handful of important Missouri producers of church windows. St. Joseph Art Glass was founded by Paul Wolff, a German who emigrated from Stuttgart in 1889. Hopcroft Art and Stained Glass was founded in Kansas City in 1914. St. Louis remained the center of the business in the state, however, having one-half to two-thirds of the companies at any given time. St. Louis companies producing church windows included Century Art Glass, Unique Art Glass and the companies of A. H. Wallis, E. F Kerwin, and William Davis. These companies also were important producers of decorated windows for the homes of the city's wealthy. The most important St. Louis producers of church windows have been the companies founded by Herman Jacoby in 1896 and Emil Frei Sr. in 1900. Numerous windows produced by these two firms remain in Missouri's churches today, including many completed in the early years of this century.

Gethsemane, First Lutheran, St. Joseph, St. Joseph Art Glass.

Although the total value produced by Missouri companies never approached that of New York and Pennsylvania, the best Missouri stained glass windows compare favorably to those produced anywhere in the United States. Because companies employed numerous designers and other workers over the many years they were in existence, the quality and style of the windows produced have varied considerably. While Robert Harmon worked at the Emil Frei company, he knew men working for other companies that "wore [their workers] out and threw them away like old shoes."

Working conditions varied from company to company. A factory inspection in 1892 noted the poor lighting and ventilation at the Kerwin company, while others received better reports. The businesses faced many of the same problems faced by other industries. In the 1890s the work week was typically six ten-hour days. Stained glass workers in St. Louis organized into a union in 1900, and the length of the work week quickly became an issue. Glass workers used the same methods for achieving their goals as workers all over America, including strikes. A strike of the St. Louis glass workers in 1902 won an agreement to shorten the work day to nine hours with only a half-day of work on Saturday. The strike lasted for twenty days and involved about 125 workers.

In addition to labor difficulties, stained glass companies also faced fluctuations in demand for their products. To some extent, these fluctuations reflected changing tastes in church architecture. However, changes in the U.S. economy were even more important influences. During the first three decades of the 20th century the demand was high as the economy prospered. New churches were built and older churches replaced their clear windows with stained glass. The Great Depression of the 1930s hit the stained glass business hard, as it did many other industries. Little new work was available as churches found themselves in financial difficulty. Some work that had been completed, such as the 1929 installation of the beautiful windows of Missouri United Methodist Church in Columbia by Jacoby, could not be paid for until years later. Many companies failed in those hard times. According to one source, the Emil Frei company survived the 1930s, in large measure, because they were able to complete and be paid for designing and installing the windows in St. Francis Xavier, the church of St. Louis University.

Opposite Page: St. Nicholas, St. Nicholas Greek Orthodox, St. Louis, Unique Art Glass, 1960-1965.

Following the Depression and World War II, times remained hard for the surviving companies. Churches built in the last half of the century were designed in ways that made traditional stained glass windows inappropriate. Windows often became smaller and less prominent in the buildings and some companies were unable to adapt. Those that survived often changed dramatically as they passed from owner to owner.

The traditions of the craft are carried on in Missouri today by a variety of studios, ranging from one person operations that work only within a very small geographic area providing residential windows or even household decorations to others that continue the traditions of stained glass designs for church windows. In St. Joseph, after Paul Wolff's death his firm also died and was later resurrected as the Tobias studios, run by a former employee. Today Rick Rader's much smaller Tobiasson Stained Glass Studio represents a new generation with family ties to the Tobias/Wolff legacy. In Kansas City, Rick Hoover is reviving Hopcroft Art Glass after a long period of decline. Century, Unique and Frei all continue to operate in St. Louis. Although the traditions in which these artists work are much different from those at the beginning of this century, they continue to produce high quality stained glass windows.

Death of St. Joseph, St. Thomas the Apostle Catholic, St. Thomas, c. 1940. Notice the carpenter tools on the wall.

Opposite Page: St. John the Evangelist, Missouri United Methodist, Columbia, Jacoby, 1929.

From Generation to Generation:
Emil Frei Associates

Buildings, like the gospel, beckon us beyond where we are.
Good liturgical space calls us to heightened listening,
clearer seeing, more engaged participation.

— The Church for Common Prayer:
A Statement on Worship Space for the Episcopal Church

Certainly the most highly respected company among the Missouri stained glass firms is Emil Frei Associates. The story of this company may be the most intriguing one in the business in Missouri. After studying painting at the art academy in his home town of Munich, Bavaria, in the newly united German empire, Emil Frei came to the United States in the 1890s. He first came to New York, where he was joined by his fiancee, Emma Mueller. The two were married there, and soon moved to San Francisco, where Frei was commissioned to paint several murals. According to a family source, he and his wife were unhappy there, and they determined that they would return to Bavaria. They journeyed to St. Louis in 1898, stopping to visit friends before setting off for New Orleans where they would take ship for home. They found the city to be so German that it felt like home, and

Previous Page: The Holy Ghost, From a Trinity Window, St. Simon Cyrene Catholic (Formerly St. Philip Neri), St. Louis, Frei, 1932.

they stayed. Martha Clevinger's introduction to the Emil Frei Collection at the Missouri Historical Society tells a different story. She reports that Frei had done some work in stained and painted glass in San Francisco and was consequently invited to St. Louis to design windows for the new college church of St. Louis University.

Regardless of what brought him to St. Louis, Frei first worked as an artist for the Wallis company. In 1900 he and Emma opened Emil Frei Art Glass, Co. and operated it together until she retired in 1930. Very quickly the company entered the national arena. In 1904, windows the company designed for a church in Watertown, New York, won a grand prize at the Louisiana Purchase Exposition. Frei opened a studio in Munich about 1910, although relatively few Missouri church windows came from the German branch of the company. In fact, more work was probably done in the St. Louis studio and sent to Europe than the reverse. Surprisingly, the Munich branch remained in business through World War I and only closed with the onset of World War II. Frei was also interested in mosaics, and according to some sources, it is in this field that he made his most important artistic contributions. In the 1920s he designed mosaics for the new Cathedral Basilica of St. Louis. In 1924, the family opened Ravenna Mosaics, a company that continued the mosaic work. Artistically, Emil Frei worked within the traditions of Munich stained glass and relied heavily on glass blown in Germany for his windows.

Emil Frei Jr. was born in 1896 in San Francisco and studied art at Washington University in St. Louis before joining the firm in 1917. One of his chief artistic interests was the vivid colors and medallion designs of 13th century European church windows. This influence is easily seen in his major works, including the brilliant windows of St. Francis Xavier Church at St. Louis University and the clerestory windows of St. Charles Borromeo Church in St. Charles. Emil Jr. led the company for twenty years following the death of his father in 1942.

Another major artistic shift occurred within the company as younger St. Louis artists joined the firm. The first artistically modern windows created by the company were the work of Robert Harmon in 1938 for St. Mark's Episcopal Church. Following World War II the loss of the Munich studio also contributed to the declining interest in Munich style windows in the St. Louis company. Along with Harmon, artists including Rodney Winfield, Julius Gewinner and Francis Deck led the

Jesus and Children, Ursuline Academy Catholic, Ironton, Frei, c. 1910.

national movement toward more modern designs in stained glass. By the end of Emil Jr.'s leadership of the company in 1963, Emil Frei, Inc. was recognized as a particularly innovative studio. According to one scholar at the time, "Some of the most advanced and experimental work being done in the country today can be found in the St. Louis studios of Emil Frei. There, nothing seems impossible in either the field of design or the use of materials."

Emil Jr.'s son Robert took over control of the company in 1963, and his interest in experimental techniques and secular uses of stained glass led the firm in new directions. After the death of his father in 1967 and the departure of Robert Harmon and Julius Gewinner, he also became the artistic leader. Modern abstract designs continued to be the norm for windows designed during Robert's two decades at the helm. In 1990, his son, Stephen, assumed control of the firm, although Robert continues to be active as a designer. Stephen's brother David joined the studio in 1994, and Aaron and Nicholas, Stephen's sons, represent the family's fifth generation within the firm. The studio remains a vibrant mix of talent, with as many as fifteen projects underway simultaneously, creating stained glass windows for buildings in Missouri and around the country. Older artists such as Winfield continue their work in the firm, and it seems likely that the newest generation will leave its unique mark on the windows of Missouri's churches.

Dunn and Nagel, Detail From Christ the Friend, St. Mark's Episcopal, St. Louis, Frei (Designed by Robert Harmon), 1938. Frederick Dunn and Charles Nagel were the church architects. This window is a pun on their names. "Dunn" means "hammer" in German and "Nagel" means "nail."

Previous Page: Mary Queen of Heaven, St. Charles Borromeo Catholic, St. Charles, Frei, c. 1940.

Gethsemane and Calvary, Calvary Episcopal, Louisiana, Frei, c. 1970.

History of the Written Word, DuBourg Hall, St. Louis University,
Frei (Designed by Rodney Winfield), c. 1995. (Photographs Courtesy
of Emil Frei Associates.)

Sacred Heart, Immaculate Conception Catholic, Old Monroe, Frei, 1906.

Chapter 9
Of Irish Saints &
Confederate Sympathizers:
Windows into Missouri History

Truth has no time of its own. Its hour is now—always.

— Albert Schweitzer

Joanne Hines says she especially likes the beautiful angels in the "Sacred Heart" and "Immaculate Conception" windows in her church. She visits other churches and likes to see their stained glass windows, but, "Nobody has windows as pretty as ours," she says proudly. When Hines looks at the windows in Immaculate Conception Church in Old Monroe, where she grew up and where her family has lived for generations, she sees not only the beauty of the glass and the religious imagery, but also history: the history of her church, her community and her family. The windows donated by her grandparents and great-grandparents bear a living witness to the life of her family in the parish.

To someone who looks carefully at the stained glass windows in Missouri's churches, they provide an avenue for discovery of the state's past. Whether one is looking at a window depicting saints, biblical scenes, figures from church history or scenes from Missouri's past, they tell us something about who we are as a people. The memorial inscriptions give us glimpses into the ethnic make-up of communities as well as insights into socioeconomic factors within communities. The windows can tell us about language persistence in immigrant communities and economic ties to larger ethnic communities and even to their nations of origin.

Immigrants brought with them their religious values and traditions as well as the rest of their culture to America. Often German communities in the Missouri are laid out in the same patterns as their home villages in the German states. Many are string villages, long narrow settlements alongside a main road. The churches in these towns tend to be placed on the highest suitable building site, making them the most prominent buildings. St. George Catholic and St. Paul's United Church of Christ, the two historic churches in Hermann, sit high on hills overlooking the Missouri River. The first glimpse of Hermann a visitor approaching along the river will have is the two steeples rising high above the valley. Even in villages not settled on prominent hills, such as Old Monroe and St. Thomas, the church is built on a rise in the rolling terrain, visible from a long distance. This placement of the church is both practical and symbolic. Standing high above the surrounding countryside, the church bells could be heard for miles, calling people to prayer and services. For many who grew up in Catholic communities, the sound of the Angelus bells ringing at noon was a familiar and integral part of life.

The physical prominence of the building reflects the church's importance in the life of the people. In many places, the church was both the religious and social center of community life.

Cardinal Glennon, Sacred Heart Catholic, Poplar Bluff. Glennon was a leader in the Missouri Catholic church during the 20th century.

St. Anthony of Padua, St. Ambrose Catholic, St. Louis.

Sometimes the location of the church can teach us something unexpected about local history. Not all towns were settled by people united in a common religious faith. In some parts of the state, communities grew up around crossroads or along railroads. In these places the early inhabitants did not share a common ethnic background. There were also communities founded which did share common values that were not primarily religious. In Augusta the location of Immaculate Conception Catholic Church over a mile outside the town reportedly reflects the animosity at least some of the early German settlers in the village felt toward their fellow-German, but Catholic, farm neighbors.

Inside, the churches also reflect the immigrant culture. Familiar saints appear in windows. While St. Joseph can be found in windows of almost any ethnic group, where but in German communities would one find St. Kunigunda or St. Conrad portrayed? Where but in a community of German farmers would we see St. Gertrude with the mouse scurrying up her staff? It is not surprising that Joan of Arc appears in Ste. Genevieve where the earliest settlers were French, not in German communities. Some saints transcend their original ethnic ties to appear

Exterior, Sacred Heart Catholic, Rich Fountain.

St. Brigid, St. Patrick Catholic, St. Patrick, State Art Glass, Dublin, Ireland, 1950. St. Brigid is patroness of Ireland.

in many churches. St. Anthony of Padua is present in the windows of St. Ambrose in the Italian community in St. Louis, but elsewhere as well, and some, like St. Patrick, have become almost universal.

In addition to ethnic background, occupation sometimes played a role in the selection of window subjects. Although he was a Spaniard, St. Isidore, patron of farmers, appears in German churches in Rich Fountain and Westphalia, and we find him alongside Wendelin and Zita in Augusta. St. Wendelin was a shepherd from the area near Trier in southeastern Germany. He became a Benedictine monk and later an abbot. St. Zita is a patron of servants. She was a household servant for the same family for 48 years. In Westphalia the presence of St. Hubert, patron of hunters, is an indication of the economic importance of that activity. These saints reflect the humble origins of many of the original inhabitants in these rural communities. More modern windows in First Presbyterian Church in both Cape Girardeau and Columbia represent various professions for which the local universities prepare students.

St. Zita, Immaculate Conception Catholic, Augusta.

Previous Page: Wedding Feast at Cana, St. John Nepomuk Catholic, St. Louis, Frei Munich Studios, 1929. St. John Nepomuk was founded as a Czech/Bohemian parish. The embroidery on the groom's jacket is typical of Bohemian needlework.

St. Hubert and St. Helena, St. Joseph Catholic, Westphalia, Frei, 1905.

Previous Page: St. Isidore, Sacred Heart Catholic, Rich Fountain, Frei, 1920s.

Some windows also comment on contemporary events and issues. One particularly noteworthy example is St. Mark's Episcopal Church in St. Louis. The small simple church was built in 1938 in a quiet neighborhood. Much of the rest of the world at the time was not quiet, however, and the windows tell part of the turbulent story of the times. While the windows on one side of the nave recount the story of the life of St. Mark, those on the other side comment on social and political issues. Designed by Robert Harmon in his early years with Frei, the windows provide commentary on major issues through images not usually associated with church windows. One depicts striking workers while another shows bones, skulls, soldiers marching and bombs falling. They present moving statements on the economic troubles of the Great Depression and the violence in Europe that would culminate in World War II.

Language is one important part of immigrant culture, which is sometimes maintained for several generations, and the languages of the window dedications provide evidence of this fact. The first church in Old Monroe was built in the 1860s by German immigrants, but the stained glass windows of the present church were not installed until 1906-1918, two generations later. However, the language was still German. For example, two windows in the choir loft were donated by the *Caecilien Saengerchor* (St. Cecelia's Choir). Old Monroe is not the only place where we find German inscriptions in the windows. They are common in numerous German communities. In the Church of the Immaculate Conception in Arnold, for example, one window depicting St. Joseph bears the inscription *Gestifted von St. Joseph Maenner Verein* (given by the St. Joseph's men's organization).

Inscriptions bear witness to cultural diversity in early Missouri. In Ste. Genevieve Catholic Church in Ste. Genevieve, window dedications appear in French, the language of the first European settlers in the area, in German, reflecting the later German immigration to Missouri, and in English. Polish and Italian churches have windows dedicated in the language of their original members. At St. Nicholas Greek Orthodox Church in St. Louis, English is the language of the memorial inscriptions while Greek is used to identify the subject matter of the 1940s windows.

The languages represented are not simply "dead" languages today, although relatively few of the younger generations speak them. A visitor to the office at St. Nicholas will overhear lively conversations in Greek, English and both languages at once. St. Ambrose parish in St.

Louis holds Mass in Italian one Sunday each month, and visitors strolling the neighborhood streets will hear Italian spoken. Several German churches continue to hold some services in German. New Hispanic congregations continue that tradition in some parts of the state with services in Spanish.

Window inscriptions tell us other history. In St. Paul's Episcopal Church on the edge of Country Club Plaza in Kansas City, a window bears the dedication: "For twelve years untiring ministry 1905-1917 this parish remembers with gratitude to God this loving rector, Jefferson Davis Ritchey, August 2, 1861 - June 24, 1919." Born less than four months after the opening shots of the American Civil War were fired at Fort Sumter, he was named for a patriotic hero of the moment in the South, Confederate President Jefferson Davis. The dedication is a reminder of the close ties of much of the Episcopal Church in America with the political and religious values of the ruling class of the pre-Civil War South.

Windows relate stories of local history. A window in Second Presbyterian Church in Kansas City shows the church building and the preaching of the first Presbyterian sermon in Kansas City. A window in the Christian Church in New Franklin is known as the "MKT Window" because it was given by the railroad association, the railroad being an important employer in the town for many years. Sometimes the stories are eloquent and poignant. In Hannibal's Trinity Episcopal Church a window of "Jesus and the Children" is dedicated to Tullie Mae Davis, 1884-1887. At St. James Catholic Church in St. Joseph, two windows were given in memory of a brother and sister killed in an automobile accident. The brother is commemorated in a window depicting St. Joseph with the young Jesus, while the sister is remembered by a window of Mary, the mother of Jesus, as a girl with her mother, St. Anne. At University Heights Baptist Church in Springfield, a former member of the congregation, Eddie Mathews, was a star athlete, playing and later coaching basketball at Southwest Missouri State. After his sudden death from a heart attack, a memorial window was created showing him going for a lay-up. The message, according to a church brochure, is that "whatever we do in life... we may do for the glory of God."

Taken as a whole, Missouri's stained glass windows comprise a treasure of art, culture and history. In Old Monroe, Joanne Hines is concerned about the future of the windows, however. Maintenance and restoration are expensive. The parish held an auction to raise money for

St. Patrick, St. Patrick Catholic, Rolla, Frei c. 1905. In addition to being the patron saint of Ireland, St. Patrick is also the patron saint of engineers.

needed work several years ago. She worries about whether the younger generations will care as much about the windows as her generation does. "They like more modern things," she comments.

The parish showed the value it places on its heritage when restoration work was underway on the church in the mid-1990s. Workers discovered that the English inscriptions on the statuary representing the Stations of the Cross were written on tape, not on the statuary itself. When the tape was removed, they discovered older German inscriptions underneath. In a parish meeting, the members of the church voted to return to the original German, complementing the German inscriptions on the windows.

Hines is right to be concerned about the future of the windows. Maintenance needs are on-going and restoration work is inevitable and expensive. Priests, ministers and congregations around the state lament their inability to preserve what they have. Other churches stand empty and unused. Without a significant commitment, many of these very valuable windows will be lost, and with them an important part of Missouri's cultural heritage.

Kateri Tekakwitha, Sacred Heart Catholic, Valley Park. Kateri
Tekakwitha was a young Native American woman who was a
17th cntury convert to Christianity.

Creation, Wyatt Park Christian, St. Joseph, Frei, 1957. A stream of light flows from its source at the top, down on the left, and on the right a second shaft of light returns. The window's central message is that man must accept the gifts God has created and offer them back in prayer, praise and worship. This window, approximately 20' x 40', dominates the church interior.

Chapter 10

In the House
of the Lord

O Lord, I love the habitation of thy house,
and the place where thy glory dwells.

— Psalms 26:8

R uss Collins likes to bring people into his church, Happy Zion
General Baptist in Annapolis, and show them the windows
designed by Robert Harmon. Compared to Roman Catholic or
Episcopal traditions, Baptist churches are less likely to present a wide
range of traditional iconography. Many symbols common in the
religious art of Europe are uncommon there. The images of Harmon's
windows speak to the experience of the Ozarks congregation. His work
is filled with the plants, stones and water that surround them, and these
images form a part of the stories of Jesus' life that the windows
illustrate. Harmon's windows speak even to one unfamiliar with the
long tradition of Western religious art. Collins finds that they provide a
way to bear witness of his Christian faith to others and to tell them the
New Testament story by guiding them around the series of windows.

Collins is not alone in his use of windows as teaching tools. In
churches as distant as Zion Lutheran in Palmyra and Ste. Genevieve
Catholic in Ste. Genevieve we hear of sermons based on the stories or
saints found in the windows. In countless Sunday School or
confirmation classes teachers instruct their pupils on the lessons to be
learned from the windows in their churches. However, the religious

Nativity, Happy Zion General
Baptist Church, Annapolis,
Harmon, 1999.

impact of stained glass windows goes beyond the subject matter they present. The simple beauty of the light that they transmit enriches the spiritual experiences of those within the church.

In St. Joseph Dwight Dannen recalls his family's involvement with the huge window that lights the sanctuary of Wyatt Park Christian Church. The architect's original plans for the church called for a window with "big rectangular panes of glass," but it did not seem "artistic" to Dannen's family. They decided to donate a more suitable window that would be more beautiful and religious as a memorial to his father. When Robert Frei first presented his modern design, however, Dannen and the rest of his family were not pleased. The window design seemed "frivolous" with "no purpose to it." It appeared abstract and without meaning. They asked Frei to come up with another design, but "it was worse," Dannen says. Although the church eventually decided to proceed with the installation of Frei's original design, the members of the Dannen family showed their displeasure by refusing to dedicate the window to their father and by shifting their contribution to the building fund rather than paying directly for the window.

Dannen says his sister, who was especially displeased with it, never changed her opinion, but he did. When he first saw the window more than forty years ago, it seemed to him to have "no rhyme or reason," but once Frei had explained the intent and the meaning of the symbols, it made sense. When the sun comes through that south window on a Sunday morning, he says, he likes to watch it move across the floor as the service progresses. Sometimes a person participating in the service will be "bathed in the light" of a particular color. An elderly woman showing a visitor around the church comments that she finds the window inspirational. Without the more obvious content of Harmon's Happy Zion windows, Frei's Wyatt Park window contributes significantly to the life of the church.

In much the same reverential tones, a woman speaks of the abstract Frei window in Campus Lutheran Church in Columbia. "When I see the light coming through that window on Easter morning," she pauses, "It just wouldn't be Easter without it." In her eyes, the light of the risen sun represents the light of the risen Christ. The window needs no images to convey this spiritual message.

When we hear comments like these, little seems to have changed since the days of Roger of Helmershausen almost 900 years ago. We still "consider the light streaming through the windows... [and] marvelleth at the priceless beauty of the glass and at the variety of this most precious work."

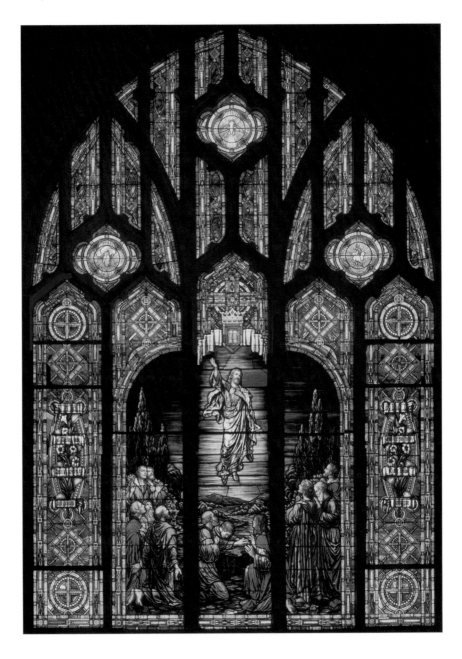

Ascension, Broadway United Methodist, Kansas City. Photograph by Carl James.

Photography Tips

In our travels around the state to inventory and photograph church windows, we met a number of people who had photographed the windows in their own churches. Often they were dissatisfied with the results. We'd like to offer some basic tips to those who are brave enough to try to capture on film the glory of light streaming through a window. With some basic equipment—a 35 mm camera and a tripod—it will often be possible to take excellent photos.

There are many good reasons to photograph the windows in your church: the photographs could be used in a church history book, put on a postcard for visitors, or included in a church web site. Perhaps most importantly, it is a good idea to have a photographic record as a kind of insurance. If a window is damaged—and unfortunately such things happen, most commonly from natural disasters and vandalism—a photograph could be invaluable to the restoration of the window.

First, visit a camera store and ask someone to recommend a professional quality film designed to maximize color saturation. Almost all of the photographs in this book were taken with Fujichrome Velvia.

Second, turn off all lights inside the building. Any light reflected off the inside of the windows reduces the amount of outside light the camera registers. It is the outside light that is essential.

Third, always use a tripod. You will need to use very slow shutter speeds to capture the necessary amount of light.

Fourth, experiment with different light settings. The amount of light coming through a window varies tremendously depending on the glass used in the window and the amount of sunlight outside the window. In general, you should slightly underexpose the picture for the best color, although we recommend taking several shots of the same window at different camera settings so that some will be overexposed and some underexposed. Try photographing at different times of the day. A window in direct sunlight may be impossible to capture on film. We often got the best results on overcast days. Keep a record of your camera settings for each shot. That way you can study the results and learn from your experience.

Don't be discouraged. Remember that professional photographers expect only a small percentage of their field shots to be good quality. Don't expect more of yourself.

St. George, Ursuline Academy Catholic, Ironton.

Stained Glass Tours

Churches are not museums, and generally, they are not set up to receive casual visitors who want to drop by to study or admire their windows. Unfortunately, because of vandalism and other threats, many churches keep their doors locked except for scheduled events. However, this does not mean that it is impossible to see some of Missouri's great wealth of stained glass windows.

First, in St. Joseph, there is a church building that is now a museum. Twin Spires, a museum of St. Joseph's multi-faith religious history, has some very fine Munich style windows designed by the Frei company. Twelve windows in this former Catholic church depict the life of Mary, a fairly unusual subject.

Second, some churches do open their buildings to the public and welcome visitors. For example, St. Francis Xavier, the college church of St. Louis University, is open during the week, as is Christ Episcopal Cathedral in St. Louis, which provides materials for visitors to take a self-guided tour of the historic building, including the windows. In the Cathedral, one can see a great variety of artistic styles in stained glass. The Cathedral has some of the oldest windows in Missouri, some English and Belgian windows, windows by well-known American artists such as Charles Connick and Louis Tiffany, and modern windows by Missouri designers. Stop by the bookshop or office to pick up your self-guided tour booklet.

Third, all churches welcome visitors to attend services. This can be a particularly rewarding way to see stained glass windows, because it is possible to more fully appreciate how the windows contribute to the church's religious tradition. As you take weekend trips around Missouri, consider adding a church service to your agenda. It's a great way to see some of Missouri's architecture and art and learn about its religious traditions.

There really are no rules, per se, for visiting churches to look at windows beyond basic courtesy, but a few suggestions might be helpful:

1. If you don't know whether a church building is open for visitors, call and ask. If possible, attend a service. You'll be welcomed and will probably find someone you can talk with about the windows afterwards.

2. Don't disrupt a service by wandering around looking at windows. Participate and study the windows later.

3. Be sensitive to the needs of the congregation or parish. If a service is about to begin or the building is being used for another purpose, find a more appropriate time to visit.

4. Speak quietly and be aware that some churches ask for silence to be kept in the sanctuary.

5. Dress conservatively. Denominations differ in terms of what would be considered appropriate attire in the church building, but be aware that shorts, tank tops and similar clothing might be offensive in some traditions.

6. If you want to take photographs, first ask for permission.

Confirmation, Missouri
United Methodist, Columbia.

Regional Favorites

U se this book as a guide to help you decide which churches you might be most interested in visiting. Here are a few of our personal favorites from around the state. Collectively, they represent some of the best of the various stained glass artistic traditions in Missouri churches. Remember that there are many churches with excellent windows that are not included in this book.

Central Missouri — Sacred Heart in Rich Fountain, St. Joseph in Westphalia, and St. George in Hermann all have Frei windows in styles typical of the German Catholic churches. Missouri United Methodist Church in Columbia offers good examples of medieval-style iconography.

Kansas City — Second Presbyterian has a variety of styles, including figured opalescent windows by Tiffany and Lamb, and beautiful red and blue Willet windows placed typologically. Grace and Holy Trinity Episcopal Cathedral and St. Paul's Episcopal also have a variety of styles. Our Lady of Perpetual Help Redemptorist Catholic has some very interesting Frei Munich style windows. Immaculate Conception Catholic Cathedral's windows are some of the oldest in the city.

St. Louis — Missouri's oldest city has the largest amount of old stained glass. Literally dozens of churches are worth visiting. In addition to those included in this book, St. Alphonsus Liguori (Rock) Catholic has Mayer of Munich windows from 1904, Grace Methodist has windows by Tiffany, Jacoby and Frei, and for those who want to see more Tiffany windows, Second Presbyterian has eleven. Many smaller communities outside the city have churches worth visiting as well.

Southeast — Ste. Genevieve Catholic in Ste. Genevieve has the oldest windows in the area. While you are there, be sure to look at the wonderful wooden choir stalls with carvings of Kateri Tekakwitha and Elizabeth Ann Seton among the twelve apostles, four church fathers and Jesus. St. Cecelia Catholic in Kennett has some of the finest faceted glass we found, and Kennett's old Protestant churches in the downtown area have an interesting assortment of windows. St. Vincent de Paul Catholic and St. Mary Catholic Cathedral in Cape Girardeau have excellent modern windows.

Southwest — Freistatt, an old German Lutheran settlement, has a beautiful white stone church with modern faceted glass. Joplin and Carthage have a number of historic churches. St. Philip's Episcopal in Joplin is another white stone church with excellent windows. Be sure to look at the windows along the corridor between the church and the Parish House. These are very reminiscent of the English church tradition.

Northeast — The tiny village of St. Patrick is proud of its Irish heritage, evident in its 37 church windows that were made in Ireland and include many Irish saints. Calvary Episcopal in Louisiana and Trinity Episcopal in Hannibal have excellent Frei windows, and Calvary has a wonderful Last Supper by Whitefriars. Zion Lutheran in Palmyra has good examples of painted rather than stained glass.

Northwest — St. Joseph was home to many German immigrants, and that fact is evident in its church windows. Certainly Twin Spires Museum is a must see, but check out some of the neighborhood churches. Most of the older ones are near each other in the downtown area. While you are in this part of the state, stop in some of the smaller towns to see what the churches there have. Absolutely do not miss Conception Abbey in Conception—although the stained glass there is not remarkable, the mosaics are—and the Benedictine Chapel of Perpetual Adoration in nearby Clyde, where the nuns will be glad to give you a guided tour if you make arrangements ahead of time.

Index

Annapolis
    Happy Zion General Baptist Church 74, 121, 122, 123
Arnold
    Church of the Immaculate Conception Catholic 116
Augusta
    Immaculate Conception Catholic Church 110, 113
Cape Girardeau
    First Presbyterian Church 46, 113
    St. Mary Catholic Cathedral 40, 130
    St. Vincent de Paul Catholic Church 53, 130
Carthage
    First Christian Church 68
    Grace Episcopal Church 57
Charleston
    St. Henry Catholic Church 9
Clyde
    Benedictine Chapel of Perpetual Adoration 69, 130
Columbia
    Campus Lutheran Church 11, 123
    First Presbyterian Church 113
    Missouri United Methodist Church 66, 94, 97, 128, 129
Conception
    Conception Abbey 130
Freistatt
    Trinity Lutheran Church 22, 130
Hannibal
    Trinity Episcopal Church 28, 117, 130
Hermann
    St. George Catholic Church 4, 16, 108, 129
    St. Paul's United Church of Christ 108
Independence
    First Christian Church 90

Ironton
Ursuline Academy Catholic Church 101, 126
Jefferson City
Grace Episcopal Church 21, 51
Immaculate Conception Catholic Church 24
St. Peter's Catholic Church 12
Joplin
St. Philip's Episcopal Church 36, 130
United Hebrew Temple 29
Kansas City
Broadway United Methodist Church 124
Grace and Holy Trinity Episcopal Cathedral .. 10, 32, 33, 82, 83, 129
Immaculate Conception Catholic Cathedral 129
Our Lady of Perpetual Help Redemptorist Catholic Church 129
St. Paul's Episcopal Church 3, 45, 117, 129
Second Presbyterian Church 50, 117, 129
Unity Temple on the Plaza 47, 63
Kennett
First Baptist Church 30
First Presbyterian Church .... back coverleaf
St. Cecelia Catholic Church 56, 130
Kimmswick
St. Joseph Catholic Church .... cover, frontispiece, 78
Louisiana
Calvary Episcopal Church 14, 104, 130
St. Joseph Catholic Church 60
New Franklin
Christian Church 117
New Madrid
Immaculate Conception Catholic Church 68
Old Monroe
Immaculate Conception Catholic Church 106, 107, 108, 116, 117-118
Palmyra
Zion Lutheran Church 48, 121, 130
Poplar Bluff
Sacred Heart Catholic Church 108
Potosi
Potosi Presbyterian Church 18
Rhineland
Church of the Risen Savior Catholic 7, 84
Rich Fountain
Sacred Heart Catholic Church 71, 110, 113, 114, 129
Rolla
St. Patrick Catholic Church 118
St. Charles
St. Charles Borromeo Catholic Church 67, 100, 102

St. James
    Trinity Episcopal Church 39, 85
St. Joseph
    Christ Episcopal Church 6, 8, 38, 87
    First Lutheran Church 93
    Francis Street Methodist Church 31, 86-89
    St. James Catholic Church 117
    Twin Spires Museum 54, 127, 130
    Westminster Presbyterian Church 73
    Wyatt Park Christian Church 120, 123
St. Louis
    Cathedral Basilica of St. Louis 100
    Christ Church Episcopal Cathedral 34, 64, 127
    Grace Methodist Church 129
    St. Alphonsus Liguori (Rock) Catholic Church 129
    St. Ambrose Catholic Church 109, 113, 116
    St. Francis Xavier Catholic Church 94, 100, 127
    St. John Nepomuk Catholic Church 72, 112
    St. Louis University, DuBourg Hall 105
    St. Mark's Episcopal Church 77, 100, 103, 116
    St. Nicholas Greek Orthodox Church ...... dedication page, ii, 95, 116
    St. Paul's Evangelical Church (Creve Coeur) 42, 55
    St. Simon Cyrene Catholic Church 49, 98
    Second Presbyterian Church 129
St. Patrick
    Shrine of St. Patrick Catholic 111, 130
St. Thomas
    St. Thomas the Apostle Catholic Church 37, 96, 108
Ste. Genevieve
    Ste. Genevieve Catholic Church 15, 110, 116, 121, 130
Springfield
    University Heights Baptist Church 41, 117
Starkenburg
    Shrine of Our Lady of Sorrows Catholic 35
Tipton
    St. Andrew Catholic Church .... coverleaf, 62
Valley Park
    Sacred Heart Catholic Church 119
Vienna
    Visitation Catholic Church 17, 61
Washington
    St. Francis Borgia Catholic Church 23, 65
Westphalia
    St. Joseph Catholic Church 58, 113, 115, 129

Jesus and the Children, First Presbyterian, Kennett.